Backroad Buffets
&
Country Cafes

A SOUTHERN GUIDE TO
MEAT-AND-THREES & DOWN-HOME DINING

DON O'B

DESIGN BY DEBRA LONG HAMPTON
COMPOSITION BY THE ROBERTS GROUP
PRINTED AND BOUND BY R.R. DONNELLEY & SONS

Library of Congress Cataloging-in-Publication Data

O'Briant, Don, 1943–
    Backroad buffets & country cafes : a Southern guide to the meat-and
-threes & down-home dining / Don O'Briant.
        p.   cm.
    Includes index.
    ISBN 0-89587-221-8 (alk. paper)
    1. Restaurants--Southern States--Directories.   I. Title.
TX907.3.S68027   1998
847.9575--dc21
                                                                98-39482
                                                                    CIP

Contents

Virginia

Acknowledgements

Most of the backroad buffets and country cafes in this book came from recommendations from friends, relatives, and total strangers. Everyone, it seems, has a favorite down-home place to eat. Not all measured up to what may have been distant memories, but all were interesting. I want to thank everyone who helped with suggestions and those who actually went out onto the blue highways to some of the more distant cafes. Freelance food critic Susan Miller did a wonderful job of capturing the flavor of Kentucky restaurants, just as Chris Wohlwend and Marcia Schnedler did in eastern Tennessee and Arkansas. Thanks to Associated Press reporter Jessica Saunders for sampling the food around Montgomery, Jack Betts and Kathleen Purvis of the *Charlotte Observer* for their expertise in North Carolina, food writer John T. Edge for his insights into Louisiana restaurants, bookseller Carolyn O'Brien for her help in Mississippi, *Memphis Commercial-Appeal* food and book critic Fredric Koeppel for his guidance in the Memphis area, and *Atlanta Journal-Constitution* colleagues

Jim Auchmutey, Wendell Brock, Eileen Drennan, Miriam Longino, Kent Mitchell, and Nancy Roquemore for their culinary assistance. And my gratitude to the celebrities who graciously wrote essays or called to tell me about their favorite restaurants—Tina McElroy Ansa, John Berendt, Roy Blount, Larry Brown, James Lee Burke, Robert Coram, Janice Daugharty, John Egerton, Connie May Fowler, Winston Groom, Josephine Humphreys, Michael Johnson, Jan Karon, Terry Kay, Governor Zell Miller, Willie Morris, Charles McNair, Lee Smith, Hoppin' John Martin Taylor, Calvin Trillin, Kathy Hogan Trocheck, Bailey White, and Fred Willard. Last, but not least, thanks to the crew at John Blair for their support, and to the women in my life who taught me that food could be a spiritual experience.

Introduction

In an era of fast food and chain restaurants, we forget that there are places where conscientious cooks still peel and mash potatoes, simmer fresh greens, and pan-fry chicken; where food is prepared from scratch and there are no heat lamps for precooked hamburgers.

These mom-and-pop restaurants used to be called meat-and-threes because of the lunchtime specials of an entrée and three vegetables. Every town had at least one or maybe more. It was where courthouse clerks shared a table with judges, and pulpwood workers passed the time with traveling salesmen over a plate of country-fried steak and a bowl of collards.

You have to look hard to find such places now, but they're still out there, somewhere between the Wal-Marts and the Burger Kings, maybe out of town a few miles. Some are absolutely wonderful, as good in their way as any gourmet restaurant. Others are, well, mediocre. The backroad buffets and country cafes you will find in this book are all pretty good, or at least pretty interesting. Some are excellent. I omitted the truly bad ones.

The list of eating establishments is purely personal and arbitrary. If I've missed your favorite restaurant, drop me a line in care of the publisher, and I'll check it out for the next edition. There is a definite scarcity of barbecue restaurants in this guide, and there's a reason for that. Any number of books have been written about such establishments, many of them in great detail. The places that serve barbecue that I've included offer other food besides barbecue or are so interesting in other ways I couldn't leave them out.

Here's what I have learned during my culinary travels through the South. People love all-you-can-eat places. There is an explosion of catfish-and-chicken restaurants and seafood buffets where you can gorge yourself for ten dollars or so. Breakfast is still one of the most dependable meals you can get on the road, and biscuits are as distinctive as fingerprints. Every cook leaves his or her mark on these baked morsels. Small, flat, well-browned ones are devoured in Tennessee and parts of Alabama, while fluffy catheads are favored in South Carolina and Georgia. Angel biscuits pop up everywhere.

Turkey and cornbread dressing is the favorite Sunday meal in almost every state in the South. There are no statistics on this, just anecdotal evidence. Fried chicken, by the way, runs a close second.

Hush puppies are a mystery and vary from state to state. Some, particularly in North Carolina, are sweet and yeasty and the shape of an index finger, while others in the South are round lumps with lots of onion bits and no sugar. All are good, except the frozen ones.

Some sad notes. Cracklin' cornbread is practically extinct. Lard is not used nearly as frequently as it used to be, much to my sadness and the glee of heart specialists. Sweet tea is not universally available in every restaurant. Otherwise reputable cafes and tea rooms are actually using canned vegetables. And in some locales, chitlins are being brazenly offered on buffet lines right alongside the baked ham and fried chicken without any identification.

The good news. While the South may be becoming homogenized in other areas, its distinctive culinary heritage is surviving. As Southern culture expert John Shelton Reed pointed out, in Carrboro, North Carolina, there's a little restaurant called Country Junction where the owners and cooks are Chinese and the customers are a melting pot from all socio-economic and ethnic classes. The one thing they have in common is a taste for good Southern vegetables at a cheap price.

In Wilson, North Carolina, a successful African-American barbecue entrepreneur told me something that rings true. Food breaks down all ethnic and social barriers. In many of the cafes, Republicans and Democrats, blacks and whites break bread together and forget their differences at least for an hour, maybe longer. It's hard to be angry with someone from another race or political party when you're both sitting in a cafe eating ribs that practically melt in your mouth.

Keeping that bit of wisdom in mind, I hope you will find *Backroad Buffets and Country Cafes* enlightening and entertaining as well as useful. It not only is a guide to where you can find good down-home cooking, seafood, and regional specialties, it is a road map to forgotten parts of the South. There are some people, I know, who prefer staying in Holiday Inns when they travel to Europe because they want no surprises. This book is not for you. This is a book for the adventurous in spirit. May you never go to bed hungry or bored.

Don O'Briant

If you would like to suggest other restaurants that feature country cooking, write:

Don O'Briant
John F. Blair, Publisher
1406 Plaza Drive
Winston-Salem, NC 27103-1470

ALABAMA

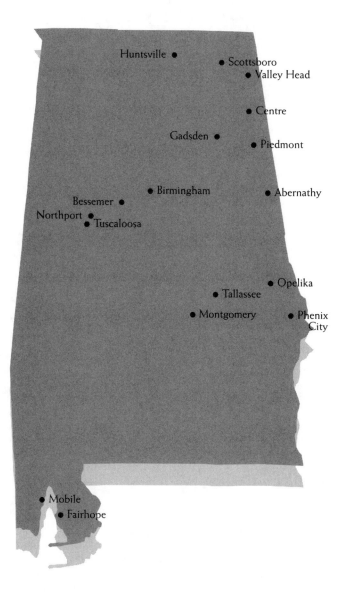

Huntsville ●

● Scottsboro
● Valley Head

● Centre

Gadsden ●
● Piedmont

● Birmingham
Bessemer ●
Northport ●
● Tuscaloosa

● Abernathy

● Opelika
● Tallassee
● Montgomery
● Phenix
City

● Mobile
● Fairhope

Abernathy

Ramburne Cattle Auction Cafe

Exit 210 off Interstate 20; go about seven miles toward Abernathy
(205-748-2171)
Hours: Monday-Thursday, 10:30 A.M.–1:00 P.M.; Friday, 10:30 A.M.–1:00 P.M. and
   4:30 P.M.–8:00 P.M.

If you don't mind eating in a cattle barn, this is a good place to have lunch. Actually, it's just in the same metal building as the weekly cattle auction. Known locally as the Sale Barn Cafe, this functional establishment serves up daily specials that include fried chicken breast, ham, catfish, pork chops, chuck-wagon steak, and an assortment of vegetables. For $3.50 you can get a meat and three vegetables and coffee or tea, and that's a real bargain, even with a herd of cattle lowing next door. By the way, and I don't know if this is a coincidence or not, but the waitress told me in confidence that their most popular meal is rib-eye steak.

Bessemer

Bright Star Restaurant

304 North 19th Street
(205-424-9444)
Hours: Monday-Saturday, 11:00 A.M.–10:00 P.M.;
   Sunday, 11:00 A.M.–9:00 P.M.

Owner Jimmy Koikos and Chef Rick Daidone

The Bright Star has been a culinary institution in this small town since 1907. Tom Bonduris took over the cafe in 1915, after arriving from Greece. Within a couple of years, his place was a favorite stop for Bessemer businessmen. The current owner, Bonduris's nephew Jimmy Koikos, has continued to build on the restaurant's reputation for serving fresh seafood and

Bright Star Restaurant

Southern favorites. Seafood is shipped in from the Gulf daily and chef Rick Daidone does the rest. You can't go wrong with any of the meat-and-three luncheon specials such as baked ham, red-snapper throats, roast beef and gravy, or Greek-style chicken. I was dubious about the snapper throats, but they are the meat left near the head after the snapper is filleted, and they are delicious.

Vegetable choices include field peas with snaps, sautéed corn, baby lima beans, steamed cabbage, potato salad, or candied yams. If you're there for dinner, I recommend any of the seafood, but especially the snapper with olive oil, lemon juice, and oregano, and a cup of the gumbo. I sampled some of the best in New Orleans, and Rick's spicy seafood gumbo is as good, if not better. For dessert, try the banana nut pie, the chocolate almond pie, or the bread pudding with whiskey sauce. You can thank me later.

Centre

Muffins 50's Cafe
Highway 411 West
(205-927-2233)
Hours: Monday-Thursday, 10:30 A.M.–9:00 P.M.; Friday, 10:30 A.M.–10:00 P.M.;
    Saturday, 11:00 A.M.–10:00 P.M.; Sunday, 11:00 A.M.–8:30 P.M.

Judy Caldwell is Muffin, and it's no secret what her favorite color is. This 1950s-style diner is pink stucco with pink parking meters out front. Inside, have a seat on a car seat with arm rests made from the tail fins of a pink 1959 Cadillac. The restaurant has three separate rooms for diners and browsers, with 1950s memorabilia such as Tinker Toys and other games scattered everywhere. In lieu of an Elvis life-size cutout, there's one of Billy Ray Cyrus. Oh, yes, Muffin also serves food that's down-home and delicious. Besides steaks, seafood, and burgers, you can order country-fried steak and pepper gravy with three vegetables for less than five dollars. Daily specials vary, but there are always more vegetables than Kooky had combs. And if you have to ask who Kooky is, you weren't around in the '50s to watch 77 *Sunset Strip* on television. A sampling of menu offerings include mashed potatoes, turnip greens, green beans, macaroni and cheese, pinto beans, steamed cabbage, zucchini and tomatoes, cucumber salad, pistachio salad (not bad), baked apples, fresh spinach, and Brussels sprouts. The specialty of the house (Muffin's favorite) is smothered chicken. And best of all, you can enjoy all of the above while listening to golden oldies.

Billy Ray Cyrus watches over Muffin's memorabilia.

Bay Springs Marina and Restaurant

Look for the sign on Highway 411 after you leave Centre, heading west toward Leesburg. It's about a quarter-mile on County Road 26.
(205-927-8322)
Hours: Monday-Sunday, 6:30 A.M.–9:00 P.M.

Centre calls itself the "Crappie Capital of the World," which sounds kind of suspicious unless you know that a crappie is a delicious freshwater game fish. Unfortunately, it is against the law to sell them, so if you don't catch your own during one of the major fishing tournaments here, you have to settle for catfish fingers, chicken fingers, or chicken livers. Add three vegetables from a selection of turnip greens, crowder peas, baked beans, slaw, French fries, or other daily specials. Other menu items include frog legs, shrimp, oysters, and blackened catfish filets. Waitress Melinda Helm has seen a lot of fishermen and fish pass through the restaurant. That's probably why her favorite meal is chicken fingers.

Fairhope

Julwin's Southern Country Restaurant
Downtown Fairhope
(334-990-9372)
Hours: Monday-Saturday, 6:00 A.M.–9:00 P.M.; Sunday, 6:00 A.M.–2:00 P.M.

Set on the Gulf Coast across the bay from Mobile, Fairhope is a picturesque little town filled with antique and craft shops, a bookstore, and more than its share of writers and artists. There are several upscale restaurants in the area, but Julwin's is the place for down-home cooking. This is the Southern equivalent of Elaine's Restaurant in New York as a literary gathering place. On any given day, you're liable to find authors Winston Groom, Fannie Flagg, W.E.B. Griffin, Terry Cline, or Judith Richards eating breakfast or sampling one of the daily specials. Steven Segal even dined here while he was filming *Under Siege*. The owners recently installed an open pit for barbecue, but you can get almost anything you want, from hamburgers and liver and onions to a delicious selection of fresh seafood. Among the specialties are steamed snapper and steamed Royal Red Shrimp, which are harvested about one hundred miles off the Gulf Coast in pollution-free waters.

Gadsden

Jim's Bar-B-Que

2413 Ewing Avenue
(205-546-9060)
Hours: Sunday-Thursday, 10:30 A.M.–8:30 P.M.; Friday-Saturday, 10:30 A.M.–9:00 P.M.
(There is a second location in downtown Gadsden, 635 Broad Street, 205-546-7008.)

I decided not to include barbecue restaurants in this book because there are a number of other guides devoted solely to that delicacy. Jim's Bar-B-Que made it because more than barbecue is served and because Jim Akin's sign caught my eye. It promised fifty dollars to anybody who could eat seven Superburgers in less than an hour. I ordered one expecting something about the size of a tennis ball. Instead I got a burger the size of a large salad plate, loaded with nine ounces of hand-shaped, freshly cooked beef, lettuce, tomato, onions, mustard, ketchup, and mayonnaise. While I was waiting for the burger to cook, I couldn't help but notice a mannequin's arm and leg hanging down from the ceiling. "That's a joke," Akin said. "It's just the air-conditioning repairman." The signs advertising fried reindeer and possum sandwiches were also jokes, he added, leaning on the counter where a large rock had been placed with the sign, "Man's First Bomb." Akin explained that the downtown diner has been in operation since 1935. During World War II, the restaurant was frequented by Mickey Rooney and Red Skelton, who were stationed at nearby Camp Sibert. In the late '50s and '60s, Alabama coach Paul "Bear"

Bryant was a frequent customer.

Akin is proud of his barbecue, but he also has daily specials of fried fish, chicken fingers, and hamburger steaks with a choice of pinto beans, fried okra, fried squash, macaroni and cheese, turnip greens, creamed potatoes, and sliced tomatoes. Still hungry? Akin will fry one of his eighteen-ounce hamburgers. If you eat three of these in one hour, they're free. What a deal!

Jim Akin and "Man's First Bomb"

Huntsville

Aunt Eunice's Country Kitchen
1006 Andrew Jackson Way N.E.
(205-534-9550)
Hours: Wednesday-Monday, 5:00 A.M.–11:50 A.M.

Breakfast is the only meal you can get at Eunice Merrell's, but that's all right. After one of Aunt Eunice's breakfasts of hot biscuits, country ham, red-eye gravy AND sawmill gravy, grits, eggs, and some of the best coffee you'll ever drink, you won't want to eat for a couple of days. Aunt Eunice and her restaurant have been institutions in Huntsville since 1952. Politicians running for any office from dogcatcher to governor know to stop in and say hello and eat a biscuit or two. And in honor of

Eunice Merrill

those sorts, there's a Liars Table in the middle of the restaurant with a sign welcoming "wimmens, biznez folk, and prechurs." I didn't sit at the Liars Table, but Aunt Eunice made me a member of the Liars Club anyway. While you're eating your biscuits, take a look at all of the pictures on the walls—everyone from Willard Scott (you don't think Willard would pass up a biscuit, do you?) and Jane Pauley to governors and astronauts. A word of caution: the restaurant is small and seating is scarce, so come early. And when you get up to pour yourself a second cup of coffee, you're expected to offer to pour everybody else one, too. It's the least you can do to help out a woman who has been up since 4:00 A.M. cooking biscuits.

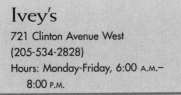

Ivey's

721 Clinton Avenue West
(205-534-2828)
Hours: Monday-Friday, 6:00 A.M.–
    8:00 P.M.

Ivey's draws downtown business people like a magnet for breakfast and lunch. The ones who aren't watching their weight get owner Barbara Swanner's favorite breakfast: two eggs, a slab of country ham, grits, gravy, home fries, or a hash-brown casserole. Daily meat-and-three lunch specials are served from a selection that includes pork chops, fried chicken, liver and onions, meat

loaf, baked ham, fish, and chicken livers. The entrées are wonderful, but the vegetables make the meal here. On almost any day, you can get fried okra, macaroni and cheese, squash casserole, creamed corn, yams, northern beans, okra and tomatoes, or turnip greens, with a choice of biscuits or cornbread.

Ivey's is spotless and roomy, just the place for a business lunch with folks who are more interested in good food than ferns and tablecloths. By the way, there is no Ivey in Ivey's. Barbara explained that when they opened the restaurant, there was a large round sign already erected for the previous business. According to the city ordinance, they had to use the same sign and find a name that would fit. "We went through the alphabet a half-dozen times," Barbara said, "and the only thing we could come up with was Ivey's. So that's what we called it."

Jackson's Family Restaurant
234 Lime Quarry Road
(205-772-0191)
Hours: Monday-Friday, 6:00 A.M.–2:00 P.M.; Saturday, 7:00 A.M.–11:00 A.M.

Take a look at the illustration of a big catfish on the Jackson's Family Restaurant menu and you'll get a hint of what the specialty is. "People love our fried catfish," says co-owner Philip Jackson. "But we're also known for our country-ham breakfasts." Both indeed are delicious. The whole catfish is fried crunchy on the outside and moist and tender inside—not mushy like some I've had. The country ham is good, too. As a matter of fact, you'd have to go a long way to find bad country ham. The Jacksons

Co-owner Philip Jackson

also offer daily meat-and-three specials such as country-fried steak and gravy, franks and kraut, and catfish along with cabbage, fried okra, vinegar slaw, corn nuggets, and pear and cottage-cheese side dishes.

The restaurant has been open since 1985, and all of the thirteen employees are family members. And as you can tell by the photographs and paintings, the whole clan obviously thought Bear Bryant walked on water.

Mobile

Tiny Diny

2159 Halls Mill Road
(334-476-3880)
Hours: Monday-Friday, 6:00 A.M.–4:45 P.M.; Saturday,
    6:00 A.M.–1:45 P.M.

When in Mobile, the temptation is to pig out at many of the fine seafood restaurants. That's all right, too, but man—and woman—cannot live on hush puppies alone. Like most cities, Mobile has a wonderful visitors information bureau with sample menus and suggestions for fine dining. But the real secret is to take one of the nice ladies at the booth aside and ask her where regular folks eat in town. In this case, the unanimous choice was the Tiny Diny.

Operated by J.L. and Trudy Shackleford, the Tiny Diny is a gastronomic jewel from the past. Friendly, big-haired waitresses serve you at Formica-top tables in a large dining room filled with folks from every socio-economic level and ethnic group. There are different specials every day, including chicken and dumplings, meat loaf, short ribs, smothered chicken,

J.L. and Trudy Shackleford

and corned beef and cabbage. If you're there on a Friday, be sure and get the salmon croquettes and potato salad. You also get a choice of three vegetables from a list of sixteen or so. And save room for dessert. The Tiny Diny has pies with meringue as high as a beehive hairdo. Miss Trudy also serves breakfasts with biscuits, grits, country ham, and red-eye gravy.

Dew Drop Inn
1808 Old Shell Road
(334-473-7872)
Hours: Saturday-Thursday, 11:00 A.M.–8:00 P.M.; Friday, 11:00 A.M.–9:00 P.M.

Another local favorite in Mobile, the Dew Drop Inn lacks the atmosphere and culinary selection of the Tiny Diny. But it's still a good place for lunch if you're in the mood for a made-to-order cheeseburger or sandwich. By all means try the chili dog. I got one just after eating at the Tiny Diny, and it still tasted juicy and delicious. Other recommendations include gumbo, homemade onion rings, jalapeño peppers stuffed with crabmeat, or a fresh fried-oyster loaf.

Wintzell's Oyster House

605 Dauphin Street
(334-432-4605)
Hours: Monday-Saturday, 11:00 A.M.–10:00 P.M.; Sunday, noon–8:00 P.M.

You want oysters, shrimp, or crab, this is one of the best places to go in Mobile. You want anything other than oysters, shrimp, or crab, better

Ernest Harris, chef at Wintzell's Oyster House

try a restaurant where they have tablecloths and soft lights and fish dishes with sauces you can't pronounce. Here you can sit at the bar, order a cold beer and steamed oysters or oysters on the half-shell, and watch while they shuck them before your very eyes. You can get hush puppies, coleslaw, and French fries, but the best way to eat oysters is the way the locals do—with saltine crackers and hot sauce. While you're slurping down oysters the size of coffee saucers, take a look at the words of wisdom that cover almost every wall in the place. ("Square Meals Make Round People," and "What the World Needs Is More Open Minds and Less Open Mouths.") Other recommendations include the gumbo and the West Indies crab salad, a Mobile original made with layers of lump crabmeat, sweet onion, oil, vinegar, and crushed ice.

Montgomery

Davis Cafe

518 North Decatur Street
(334-264-6015)
Hours: Monday-Saturday, 6:30 A.M.–10:30 A.M. and 11:15 A.M.–3:30 P.M.

By Jessica Saunders

A family-run restaurant, the Davis Cafe doesn't look like much from the outside. But don't let that turn you away. Inside is some of the best Southern-style cooking around. The fried chicken here is a delight, a slightly crispier, well-seasoned skin masking wonderfully moist, tender meat. The turkey and dressing is comfort food at its best—tasty, hearty, and satisfying. For side orders, be sure to try the fresh collard greens. The macaroni and cheese and yams are other favorites.

The Davis's menu changes daily. You can drop in on a Friday to sample the famous ribs, or a Wednesday for the fried ocean perch. Expect generous portions.

Pricewise, the Davis Cafe is a bargain. All entrées are priced the same. You pay according to the number of side dishes you order, from $3.55 for one meat and one vegetable to $5.60 for one meat and four veggies. Cornbread and tea are included. A daily selection of desserts is also available for around $1.00, but I recommend the pecan pie.

The large dining area suffers a bit from a lack of windows and dim lighting, but the yellow walls, greenery, and cheerful paintings help brighten things. One problem is parking. If you can't find a spot on the street, the next best thing is an unpaved empty lot next to the restaurant.

—Jessica Saunders is an Associated Press correspondent from Montgomery

Martin's Restaurant

1796 Carter Hill Road

(334-265-1767)

Hours: Monday-Sunday, 11:00 A.M.–3:00 P.M. and 4:00 P.M.–7:45 P.M.; Sunday,
10:45 A.M.–1:45 P.M.

By Jessica Saunders

If you like fried chicken—real, home-style fried chicken—Martin's is the place for you. Crispy, yet tender and juicy, you won't be disappointed. But chicken is only one of the things Martin's does well. Their cornbread (or you can get biscuits) could easily be the star of the show. When it arrives piping hot out of the oven, it's hard to keep reminding yourself that a full meal is on the way and to use restraint. The menu includes about a half-dozen daily specials, along with an array of side dishes and vegetables. You can always count on the fried chicken. Other offerings include country-fried steak and gravy, smoked sausage and rice, or chicken and dumplings. Some entrées are only offered at dinner, such as the popular whole fried catfish and fried chicken livers. As for vegetables, string beans, coleslaw, and some form of potato are daily staples. Other days you can get corn on the cob, collards, congealed salad, and other things. Portions are hearty, and the menu entrées average around six dollars. That includes three vegetables, a choice of bread, and iced tea or coffee. If you wind up having room, don't pass up a slice of pie, either a meringue or one of several fruit selections.

Martin's is named after the original owner, who was bought out by the late David Smith forty-one years ago. It's now owned and run by Smith's three daughters. Having been around so long, Martin's has plenty of history and tradition. Former governor George C. Wallace has been a regular visitor over the years, along with comedian Jerry Clower and local celebrity Ray Scott, founder of the Bass Anglers Sportsman's Society. Martin's has even been touched by Hollywood. Patrick Swayze used to stop by in the late 1980s, when he had a horse farm nearby.

That sense of tradition doesn't stop in the dining room. Martin's famous farm-style lunches are overseen in the kitchen by Miss Gussie Ashley, who has worked here forty years. Barbara Jackson, who bakes

the pies, has been here twenty years. The wood-paneled dining area is simple but cheerful, with lots of windows and an ample smoking section. It seats about 120 and is busiest at lunch.

—Jessica Saunders is an Associated Press correspondent from Montgomery

Northport

Northport Diner
450 McFarland Boulevard
(205-333-7190)
Hours: Monday-Sunday, 10:30 A.M.–9:00 P.M.

The Northport Diner has all of the atmosphere you would expect in a '50s-style cafe—lots of neon, comfortable counter stools and booths, and plenty of shiny stainless steel. You can get burgers and shakes here, of course, but most of the regulars order one of the Blue Plate Specials. A vegetable plate includes a choice of four from a selection of black-eyed peas, cabbage, green beans, fried okra, macaroni and cheese, mashed potatoes and gravy, pinto beans, cream corn, or turnip greens. For a dollar or two more, you can get fried chicken, pork chops, fried chicken livers, country-fried steak, fried catfish, pot roast, or fried seafood. The pot roast was on the menu the day I stopped in and was recommended by a waitress with the heavenly name of Angel Hawthorne. Her suggestion turned out to be indeed divine. I could cut the roast with my fork and the potatoes were the real thing. Desserts are also typically diner-types, too—banana splits, brownie sundaes, pecan pies, and root-beer floats. And if you happen to drive past the Northport Diner on your way to the University of Alabama, don't sweat it. The same folks own another one on 1036 15th Street in Tuscaloosa called, appropriately enough, the 15th Street Diner.

Opelika

Driving through Alabama on Interstate 85, I stopped at the Opelika exit to ask two convenience-store clerks about a good, down-home cafe. After a couple of long, blank stares, they suggested a chain steakhouse or Burger King. One young woman looked at me in wonderment. "What you want vegetables for?" I had no answer that wouldn't have insulted her, so my traveling companion and I set off to find something on our own. It was mighty slim pickin's in downtown Opelika, but we did find a recently opened place called Haynie's that was decorated like a 1950s diner with the usual rock-and-roll paraphernalia. The homemade pimento-cheese sandwiches were worth taking home to Mama, and the chicken divan, the entrée of the day, was very tasty. Desserts are still works-in-progress, and not nearly as good as the pimento-cheese sandwiches or the homemade soups. Also, a favorite of locals is the all-you-can-eat Saturday brunch with quiche, garlic cheese grits, muffins, fritters, meat-and-egg casserole, and biscuits.

Phenix City

Other Voices, Other Tastes
Chicken Comer's
By Winston Groom

In 1966, I was at Fort Benning, Georgia, and one day found myself playing tennis at the Columbus Country Club where, in those days, the dress was "all whites." Afterward, several of us and our dates decided we craved some really good barbecue. Someone suggested a place over in Phenix City, Alabama, a rough and wide-open town across the Chattahoochee River, where a few years earlier they had assassinated a candidate for governor because he was against gambling.

I had a white Jaguar sedan back then, and we all piled in and headed across the river. Following instructions, I headed along all sorts of roads for miles and miles into the countryside until the pavement played out, then continued on a dirt road where, eventually, we came upon a sign that read:

CHICKEN COMERS

BAR-B-QUE

It was nothing more than an unpainted shack with a sagging, covered porch containing an ancient Coke machine. On the steps were several red-eyed men drinking something from bottles in paper bags. They eyed us with something between suspicion and amazement. Out in the yard, among the trees, was an enormous open pit, wafting up bluish smoke. Covering the pit was something that looked to be one of those huge

sidewalk grates. On the grate several large pork roasts were cooking. On a cut-off stump beside the pit was a man who was a dead look-alike for Uncle Remus, coveralls and everything. He had a big pitchfork that he used to occasionally move or turn over one of the roasts.

The aroma was delicious.

"Well," I said to my companions, "with these get-ups, I guess maybe I'll just go in by myself." Everybody wanted two barbecue sandwiches apiece—outside cuts—and a Coke. I walked in past the red-eyed men on the steps and entered the shack.

Behind the dilapidated homemade counter were two women who blinked at me in astonishment. Behind them was a wood-burning stove, and atop it was a big kettle—what they used to call a "scalldron." A big stick protruded over the top.

I told them what I wanted, and one began laying out hamburger rolls, while the other carved off big slices of barbecue roast and laid them on the open-faced bread.

"You want sauce?" one of the women asked.

I nodded, and she turned to the scalldron and lifted the stick. On the end of the stick (and I swear this is true) was a pair of men's Jockey shorts, dripping thick reddish sauce. As I stood there speechless, she swung the stick around and dribbled the sauce over each of our eight barbecues, put pickles on top, closed the buns, wrapped them in waxed paper, and put them in a paper bag.

"How much are the Cokes?" I asked, after paying her twenty-five cents apiece for the barbecues.

"Nickel," the woman said.

I got change and took four Cokes for twenty cents out of the machine and returned to the car.

"You're not going to believe what I just saw," I said.

But as we ate our sandwiches, it was unanimously agreed that Chicken Comer, whoever he was, made the greatest barbecue of all times.

Winston Groom is the author of *Forrest Gump* and *Such a Pretty, Pretty Girl*. He lives in Alabama.

Piedmont

Frady's Gateway Restaurant

U.S. 278 Bypass and Highway 9
(205-447-9920)
Hours: Monday-Saturday, 6:00 A.M.–8:00 P.M.; Sunday, 7:00 A.M.–2:00 P.M.

Gail Frady's restaurant is a classic meat-and-three. For less than five dollars, you have a choice of a meat and three vegetables from daily specials that include fried chicken, sauerkraut and franks, veal cutlets, salmon patties, meat loaf, country-fried steak, deviled eggs, pear salad, fried okra, crowder peas, creamed corn, potato salad, squash casserole, or sliced tomatoes. Everything is prepared from scratch, including the red-velvet cake and coconut cake.

Scottsboro

Crawdaddy's Too

Goose Pond Colony (Stop in Scottsboro and ask; it's fairly remote.)
(205-574-3071)
Hours: Wednesday-Friday, 4:30 P.M.–10:00 P.M.; Saturday, 2:00 P.M.–10:00 P.M.

Just because there's a marina and golf course nearby, don't get nervous about going to Crawdaddy's Too. It's got a tin roof and a concrete floor and wooden picnic tables on a screened porch and some of the best crawfish (or crayfish) you'll ever eat. You can also get any kind of sea-food you like, including a Tramp Steamer, a combination of cajun craw-fish, snow-crab clusters, and Gulf shrimp for two for $27.50. If you'd like something more exotic, try the cajun-fried gator appetizer. Owner Ron Harrison says his cajun dishes are so popular, he plans to add more. "But people still come here for the crawfish. We sell more of them than anything else."

Tallassee

Hotel Talisi
14 Sistrunk Street
(334-283-2769)
Hours: Monday-Saturday, 11:00 A.M.–7:50 P.M.; Sunday, 11:00 A.M.–2:50 P.M.

Tallassee was not one of my scheduled stops, but I was a captive passenger in a Volvo station wagon driven by Kathy Trocheck, a mystery-writer friend who is an antique and junk collector. She's also mighty fond of fried chicken, so we veered about seven miles off Interstate 85 between Montgomery and Auburn and ended up around 1:30 in the afternoon in a town so deserted we didn't even see a dog. We did find a few late diners in the Hotel Talisi and a buffet that the late Junior Samples of *Hee Haw* would have killed for. For around seven dollars, we had a choice of fried chicken, spaghetti, beef stew, corn-bread dressing, a multitude of veg-

etables, corn muffins, and rolls. The dining room adjoins the lobby of the hotel, a gaudy Victorian place with dark, heavy furniture and colorful crimson wallpaper. The tables in the dining area are purely functional, with older waitresses who happily ignore the warning labels tobacco companies put on their products. If you go to the Hotel Talisi, take time after lunch to browse through several of the antique shops downtown. The most interesting one is The Company Store, which is located in an old stone mill a block from the hotel.

Tuscaloosa

Other Voices, Other Tastes

Archibald's

By Bailey White

My favorite place to eat is Archibald's in Tuscaloosa. They have vinegar-based barbecue, and they serve it with white bread. It's the best barbecue I've ever eaten. You know you're eating good, even if you're ignorant about barbecue.

Bailey White is the author of *Mama Makes Up Her Mind* and *Sleeping at the Starlite Motel*. She lives in Thomasville, Georgia, and does regular commentaries for National Public Radio.

The Waysider

By Charles McNair

No student at the University of Alabama ever got a real education without eating fried chicken and cloud biscuits at The Waysider. Neither did parents. An old shoeboxy house set awkwardly off the main highway that leads into old Northport, The Waysider turned out to be the perfect place to bring moms and dads who wanted to taste the honeyed university life for themselves.

Brilliant! As long as there was a meal this good in Tuscaloosa, the parents reckoned, it would be okay for their children. The Waysider drew droves of locals and four-year visitors alike; the tiny tables always seemed filled, an especially maddening predicament during the requisite half-hour wait within drooling distance of big plates laden with three-egg omelettes, grits, and fried bacon. The wait was always worth it. For starters, the coffee made the world go away . . . and everything else was gravy.

Charles McNair is a native of Alabama and the author of the novel *Land O' Goshen*.

Valley Head

Tiger Inn Family Restaurant
Commerce Street in downtown Valley Head
(205-635-6855)
Hours: Monday-Friday, 5:00 A.M.–7:00 P.M.; Saturday and Sunday, 5:00 A.M.–
 2:00 P.M.

The town of Valley Head sits at the base of Lookout Mountain and acts as a kind of funnel for campers and tourists. The Tiger Inn is a plain building a block off Highway 117. On the stormy night I stopped in, several local residents had braved the weather to take advantage of the all-you-can-eat spaghetti night. The sauce was homemade and tasty, but not as tasty as the butterfinger cake. This ought to be classified as a secret weapon. It's a German chocolate cake made with Eagle Brand condensed milk, topped with Cool Whip and pieces of Butterfinger candy bars. The orange pound cake looked mighty good, too, but I had to forgo that for another time. The Tiger Inn serves daily lunch specials of country-fried steak, ham, chicken and dumplings, pork cutlets, chicken casserole, salmon patties, and meat loaf along with a choice of three vegetables AND a dessert for $3.95. Hey, the butterfinger cake is worth that alone.

ARKANSAS

Springdale

Saint Joe

Blytheville

Wynne
Caldwell

West
Memphis

Little Rock

Scott

DeValls Bluff

Mena

Hot Springs

Benton

Hazen

Helena

Pine Bluff

Dumas

Fordyce

Marcia Schnedler, a freelance restaurant reviewer from Little Rock, wrote the entries for Ed & Kay's Restaurant, Klappenbach Bakery, Murry's, Pasquale's Tamales, Mary's Cafe and Pie Shop, Your Mama's Good Food Diner, Skyline Cafe, Ferguson Country Store, Restaurant, and Furniture Workshop, and Neal's Cafe.

Benton

Brown's Country Store & Restaurant

Exit 118 on Interstate 30
(501-778-5033)
Hours: Monday-Sunday, 6:00 A.M.–9:00 P.M.

Brown's Country Store looks like a Cracker Barrel store, but it's not. Owner Philip Brown just put some rocking chairs on the front porch, added a lot of Southern antique items, and stocked the gift shop with the same kinds of souvenirs and candy you might find in a Cracker Barrel—except for the coonskin caps. Brown's has enough coonskin caps to outfit a whole regiment of Davy Crocketts.

But forget about the souvenirs for a minute. The food is the reason you've stopped here, and it's worth the trip. Breakfast is served every morning on the buffet with a choice of biscuits and gravy, sausage, grits, eggs, pancakes, muffins, croissants, and apple butter. Well, not really a choice. You can eat all of the above if you're hungry.

The seafood buffet features boiled shrimp, battered shrimp, fried chicken, pond-raised catfish, smoked ribs, roast beef, rotisserie chicken, mashed potatoes, corn, carrots, turnip greens, black-eyed peas, cornbread, a salad bar, cobblers, cheesecake, and pies. All this on a buffet that is 100 feet long with more than 150 items.

Ed & Kay's Restaurant
Exit 116 off Interstate 30
(501-315-3663)
Hours: Wednesday-Sunday, 6:30 A.M.–9:30 P.M.

This tidy white country-style restaurant lies about halfway between Little Rock and Hot Springs, but is mostly filled by locals-in-the-know. Along with sandwiches, entrées, a salad bar, and breakfast any time of day, Ed & Kay's features daily specials that recently included Mandarin sesame chicken or a charbroiled steak patty with button mushroom gravy. Entrées come with a choice of fifteen sides that include fried okra, black-eyed or purple-hull peas, and potatoes creamed, baked, or pan-fried, plus a homemade yeast roll or corn muffin. Leave space for a piece of one of the ten or more different pies such as German chocolate, egg custard, or pineapple cream, with toppings that seem to soar at least a foot high.

Blytheville

Sharecropper's
211 West Ash Street
(501-763-5818)
Hours: Monday-Friday, 5:30 A.M.–4:00 P.M.; Saturday, 5:30 A.M.–2:00 P.M.

Blytheville is a peaceful little town with one of the best bookstores in the South. It's called, appropriately enough, That Bookstore in Blytheville, and it's a magnet for Southern authors from John Grisham to Kaye Gibbons. Sharecropper's is a magnet, too, for all the local folks and anybody else who happens to be downtown. Breakfast is served from 5:30 A.M., which is a mystery to me. I have known only a half-dozen people in my life who got up that early. Three of them were my aunts, who arose at 4:00 A.M. to milk cows and cook breakfast for my uncles, who arose at 5:30 to fortify themselves with hot biscuits and butter and grits and sausage for a long day's hunt for the elusive deer. There seemed to be quite a few deer hunters in Sharecropper's the morning I stopped in. Either that or they had an unnatural affection for camouflage.

A nearby group of regulars who looked like they were retired were solving the nation's problems. The main problem, they mumbled, was Bill Clinton. So much for favorite sons.

Breakfast at Sharecropper's is about what you would expect at a good Southern restaurant: spicy sausage, tender ham, and biscuits that are light and dunkable in the cream gravy.

Lunch at Sharecropper's is classic meat-and-three territory, with entrées such as meat loaf, liver and onions, country-fried steak, catfish, roast beef, salmon patties, roast pork, turkey and dressing, cabbage rolls, or chicken and dumplings. White beans, corn, coleslaw, green beans, and mashed potatoes are on the menu every day, with alternate choices that include macaroni and cheese, fried okra, macaroni and tomatoes, lima beans, black-eyed peas, boiled cabbage, and fried squash.

Owner Sheila Dobbs obviously does not scrimp on the quality of the food she serves. "It's all fresh and made from scratch," she said. "That's the only way to do it if you want people to keep coming here and eating."

Her customers obviously agree. The morning I was there, Sheila was celebrating her fifteenth year as owner of Sharecropper's.

Sheila Dobbs and the breakfast regulars at Sharecropper's

Caldwell

Decor inside Catfish Island

Catfish Island

Highway 1
(501-633-1706)
Hours: Monday-Thursday, 11:00 A.M.–9:00 P.M.; Friday and Saturday, 11:00 A.M.–
9:30 P.M.

If you're looking for catfish, this is the place in Caldwell. Actually, it's about the ONLY place in Caldwell. The restaurant is roomy and functional and caters to the AARP crowd, most of whom were waiting for the doors to open at 11:00 A.M. so they could eat lunch. Inside, the few attempts at decorating include some ivy along the dividers, a hornet's nest suspended from the ceiling, and deer heads mounted on each side of a carved catfish.

For about six dollars, you can get catfish fillets, fried in corn meal, with slaw, hush puppies, and French fries or baked potato. (Get the baked potato.) The catfish was delicious, but the best things on the menu are the hush puppies, the pickled green tomatoes, and the fried dill pickles. The pickled tomatoes are good enough to eat for dessert.

De Valls Bluff

Family Pie Shop

Route 70
(501-998-2279)
Hours: Wednesday-Saturday,
   9:00 A.M.–8:00 P.M.

The best way to find Mary Thomas's pie shop is to look for Craig's Bar-B-Q just outside of De Valls. The pie shop is directly across the highway from Craig's, behind a house in a white building that used to be a bicycle shop. Mrs. Thomas starts baking every day before dawn and by sundown she has baked as many as one hundred pies. Everybody has a different favorite, she told me as I squeezed into the kitchen. Two stacks of pie crusts three feet high were on the counter beside a huge black oven. She had just made some fried peach pies, and I tried one while she made a half-dozen Karo nut pies (pecan pies). Mrs. Thomas has been selling pies to the public for more than fifteen years. "Usually I make coconut, chocolate, sweet potato, and egg custard every day," she says. "But I get a lot of special orders, too, for lemon, pineapple, apple, and cherry." A whole pie costs about five dollars, except for the pecan, which is about eight dollars. "It costs more to make," says Mrs. Thomas, whose pie shop has been featured in *Southern Living* and other magazines. She says customers come from as far away as Little Rock. The peach pie, by the way, was wonderful. The pastry was flaky, and the peach filling was tart and reminiscent of the pies my grandmother used to cook.

*Mary Thomas, owner of
Family Pie Shop*

Dumas

Catfish Kitchen

217 Highway 65
(870-382-4488)
Hours: Monday-Wednesday, 11:00 A.M.–2:00 P.M.; Thursday and Friday, 11:00 A.M.–
9:00 P.M.; Saturday, 4:00 P.M.–9:00 P.M.; Sunday, 11:00 A.M.–2:00 P.M.

Dumas doesn't look like it has more than a few hundred people, and most of them seemed to be lined up for the Sunday buffet at the Catfish Kitchen. A group of black churchgoers arrived in their Sunday finery and descended upon the fried catfish and chicken with what can only be described as religious fervor. This was understandable after trying the catfish, which was crispy on the outside and moist on the inside, just like it's supposed to be. The vegetables were a little overcooked, but that's to be expected on a Southern buffet line. If you're not driving through Dumas on a Sunday, you can get a meat-and-three lunch during the week for less than five dollars. The menu varies from week to week, but usually there is fried chicken, baked chicken and dressing, pork chops, or roast beef.

Fordyce

Klappenbach Bakery

108 West Fourth Street
(870-352-7771)
Hours: Tuesday-Saturday, 6:00 A.M.–6:00 P.M.

The smell of fresh-baked breads, cookies, danishes, and desserts make your taste buds water as you pass through the bakery to get to the casual dining room. Bread and dessert lovers travel long distances to load up on goodies to keep in their freezers, breakfasting or lunching while they're at Klappenbach's. Diners can start the day with a sausage roll, cheese biscuit, a flaky French croissant, or a danish. Lunches feature the Klappenbachs' breads: a Reuben sandwich on rye, a French dip or pepper-cheese steak on a French roll, or a hot ham and cheese on a croissant. The Klappenbachs make their own chicken salad, quiches, and corned beef. It's a homey place, too. You're likely to find a lawyer-son whose office is next door, or a knee-high, third generation Klappenbach on the scene charming guests along with their grandma and grandpa, who run the place.

Hazen

Carol's Kitchen
Highway 70 and Highway 11
(870-255-4679)
Hours: Sunday–Thursday, 5:00 A.M.–8:00 P.M.; Friday and Saturday, 5:00 A.M.–
9:00 P.M.

The Carol in Carol's Kitchen was once a budding country-music singer. At least she made two 45 rpm records back in 1981 and had some publicity shots taken wearing a cowboy hat. I had not heard the songs, I don't think—"Daddy Was Right," "How Much Do Daddys Cost," "Dance Floor Love," and "Going Through the Motions"—but the records are there on the wall along with her extensive doll collection.

After giving up her music career, Carol Snider opened the cafe with her husband Herb. If you happen to be in Hazen, stop by and try the daily lunch buffet and sample the beef tips and rice, country-fried steak with white gravy, fried fish, fajitas, mashed potatoes, or other vegetables. If you're lucky, maybe Carol will sing a song for you.

Murry's

Highway 70, east of Hazen
(870-255-3266)
Hours: Tuesday-Sunday, 5:00 P.M.–9:00 P.M.

This tidy red-brick restaurant on the Mississippi Delta lies east of Hazen, which is three miles south of Interstate 40. Run by Stanley and Becky Young for eleven years, it's named for her father, Olan Murry, who learned to cook feeding the hard-working crews on Mississippi River barges (Olan and his wife, Elsie, run a hard-to-find restaurant in nearby De Valls Bluff with equally tasty Southern cooking). At Murry's, catfish is dressed daily and fried crispy-crunchy, while remaining moist and flaky inside. The restaurant also serves up deep-fried quail, steaks, hot and spicy shrimp, and seafood platters. Sides include hush puppies, creamy coleslaw, French fries, baked potatoes, and home fries with onions. Bread and yeast rolls are made on the spot, along with such desserts as bread pudding with whiskey sauce, custard and cream pies.

Helena

Pasquale's Tamales

211 Missouri Street
(870-338-6722)
Hours: Monday-Friday, 9:00 A.M.–5:00 P.M.

This is the long-term result of Italian and Mexican grandpas and grandmas trading recipes while working on a Mississippi Delta farm in the early 1900s: Luscious tamales with a high-quality beef core wrapped in creamy corn meal and corn shucks, then simmered in sauce for six hours. Spicy, succulent, and deliciously messy. The five-table eatery, just up the street from the Delta Cultural Center in this historic Mississippi River town, is attached to a small factory from which Pasquale's Tamales are shipped nationwide. This mini-melting pot also serves genuine New

Orleans-style muffaletta and other sandwiches, plus chili, beans, and New York cheesecake.

Hot Springs

Mary's Cafe and Pie Shop
432 Ouachita
(501-624-2988)
Hours: Monday-Friday, 7:00 A.M.–3:00 P.M.

This local favorite sits across from the county courthouse and within easy reach of Hot Springs's art and antiques galleries and famous Bathhouse Row from the early 1900s. Plate lunches include chicken-fried steak and two other meat entrées daily, plus such dishes as chicken and dumplings, chicken pot pie, roast beef, Salisbury steak, and baked pork chops—depending on which day you come. You'll also have a choice of sides such as mashed potatoes, beans, corn, and mixed vegetables. Soup is homemade and so is the gravy slathered over biscuits at breakfast.

McClard's Bar-B-Q
505 Albert Pike
(501-623-0713)
Hours: Tuesday-Saturday, 11:00 A.M.–
    8:00 P.M.

McClard's "wall of fame"

Yes, I know I said barbecue restaurants would not be included in this book, but it's hard to travel throughout the South without eating barbecue. Besides, the few I'm including offer items other than barbecue or are so interesting I couldn't resist putting them in the book. McClard's fits both criteria. Almost everyone I talked to in Arkansas recommended

McClard's for the barbecue and the tamales. And they were right. I ordered both the ribs and tamales and watched the waitress roll her eyes.

When they arrived, I understood why. The half-order tamale plate was enormous and covered with beans. The ribs were tender and drenched in a tangy tomato-based sauce. Everything was wonderful, but there was enough food to feed a family of four for two days.

Michelle Fryar and Greg Putman serve customers at McClard's

As I ate, the waitress pointed out the walls of fame in the restaurant and noted that this was Bill Clinton's favorite restaurant when he was in second grade in Hot Springs. And to prove that barbecue makes strange bedfellows, there was a signed picture of Mr. Republican, Newt Gingrich, on the wall just to the left of Willard Scott.

McClard's has a long history. Back in the '20s, Alex and Gladys McClard owned the Westside Tourist Court a few blocks away. When one of their down-and-out customers offered them "the world's greatest barbecue sauce" recipe in lieu of the ten dollars he owed them for the room, they accepted. When they tasted the sauce, they realized the traveler's claim wasn't exaggerated. In 1928, they opened Westside Bar-B-Que with goat as the main entrée. They moved to the present location in 1948 and offered a drive-in service with carhops. Today, the carhops are gone and so is the goat. But locked in a downtown safe deposit box is the ten-dollar recipe that started it all.

Willie's in Town

1901 Albert Pike Road
(501-623-0713)
Hours: Wednesday–Sunday, 11:00 A.M.–8:00 P.M.

With all of the Italian, Bavarian, Chinese, and fancy restaurants in Hot Springs catering to the horse-racing crowd, you had to figure there would be at least one catfish place. Willie's (there's a second location called Catfish Willie's about thirteen miles west on Highway 270 in Crystal Springs) specializes in catfish and ribs. Both Willie's have similar menus, but the Crystal Springs restaurant has roasted corn. Both have something called Pig Pie, which is a casserole consisting of layers of pork, beans, coleslaw, barbecue sauce, onions, and cheese topped with Fritos corn chips. A half-order is $2.50 and a full order is $4.95. It tastes pretty good, as long as you don't start thinking about all of the separate ingredients.

Little Rock

Doe's Eat Place

1023 West Markham
(501-376-1195)
Hours: Monday–Friday, 11:00 A.M.–2:00 P.M.;
    Monday–Thursday, 5:30 P.M.–9:30 P.M.;
    Friday and Saturday, 5:30 P.M.–10:00 P.M.

This funky skid-row restaurant is only slightly more upscale than the Doe's in Greenville, Mississippi. While power brokers and others feast on huge steaks and giant tamales in this dark and dingy watering hole, winos wander the streets outside. It's all very atmospheric. Unlike the original Doe's, which specializes in

luscious T-bone steaks and tamales, this franchise establishment also offers broiled shrimp and burgers along with the usual liquid refreshments
that grease the wheels of commerce.

Your Mama's Good Food Diner

402 South Louisiana
(501-372-1811)
Hours: Monday-Friday, 11:00 A.M.–2:00 P.M.

A traditional downtown, down-home favorite in Little Rock, Mama's
serves daily specials cafeteria style. On Mondays, for example, diners
might choose from baked lemon chicken, country-fried steak, batter-fried
pork chops, and meat loaf. Other entrées include lasagna, Coca-Cola
ham, chicken and dumplings, fried catfish, and oven-fried chicken. Sides
are fried okra, mashed potatoes, purple-hull peas, lima beans, turnips and
greens, creamed corn, and sweet potatoes. And leave room for banana
pudding, Key lime pie, pecan pie, Nieman Marcus cookies, fruit cobbler, or bread pudding with bourbon pecan sauce. The decor is quite
casual, but spruced up with old ads on the wall, including one in which
former President Ronald Reagan touts a brand of cigarettes.

Mena

Skyline Cafe

618 Mena Street
(501-394-5152)
Hours: Monday-Saturday, 5:00 A.M.–3:00 P.M.

Vacationers can sleep in and count on breakfast any time before heading out on the fifty-four-mile Talimena National Scenic Byway where
they'll find spectacular vistas as they cross the forested Ouachita Mountains to Talihina, Oklahoma. But it's also the spot where local regulars

solve the world's problems. You can't count on finding the same plate lunches and soup-and-sandwich specials each day week after week, either. One Wednesday, it might be a smothered steak with mashed potatoes, turnip greens, and pinto beans, and vegetable beef soup with a grilled ham-and-cheese sandwich. Friday is always fried catfish day, but if you have a yen on a Tuesday, owner Smitty will cook up some for you. "The other day I felt like cooking up a sack of black-eyed peas and gave 'em away," Smitty said. "Or once in awhile, I'll pick up a baloney and do a grilled sandwich with a third of a pound and cheese."

Pine Bluff

Mrs. W.R. Jones

Jones Cafe
3910 Highway 65 South
(870-534-6678)
Hours: Monday-Saturday, 6:00 A.M.–9:00 P.M.; Sunday, 11:00 A.M.–2:00 P.M.

When I stopped at a service station to ask if there were any good places to eat in Pine Bluff, the attendant didn't hesitate. "Jones Cafe right down Highway 65 is the best around." Well, I don't usually put much stock in the culinary recommendations of filling-station mechanics, librarians, or professors. I usually listen to traveling salesmen or state employees whose jobs take them out into the boondocks. In this case, however, Buck (that was the name sewed on his shirt) was right on the money. I arrived at Jones Cafe in time for a Sunday dinner of pot roast and fried chicken with fried okra, corn balls (fried clumps of cornbread with corn kernels), green beans, and purple-hull peas. The Karo pecan pie was so sinful I tried a few bites of the lemon pecan just to make sure I wasn't hallucinating. I wasn't.

After I ate, I talked to Jan Jones, the daughter-in-law of the founder, Ruby Pierce Jones, about the history of the restaurant. It seems Ruby Jones, who is in her nineties, started cooking in a boarding house at a lumber camp in Fikesville when she was fifteen. Four boxcars were pulled together to make the boarding house. When Ruby's father had to work away from the main camp, Ruby went with him to do the cooking. In 1925, Ruby married a fireman from Pine Bluff and opened a lunch grill across from the train depot. During the early years of World War II, hundreds of troops ate at the cafe while their train was stopped. When her husband retired and bought a farm, Ruby opened Jones Cafe in Noble Lake and used the vegetables, the butter, and the eggs from the farm in the restaurant. For a time, she had tomato and pepper plants out front, and customers could pick their own and bring them in for the waitress to peel and slice. In 1985, Jones Cafe moved to its present location on Highway 65 under the management of Ruby's son, W.R. and his wife, Jan. "She still gets up and comes to the restaurant by 6 A.M.," Jan says. "She'll prepare sixteen to eighteen dozen rolls and biscuits." Jones Cafe has won the *Arkansas Times* Readers Choice Award several times. Eat there and you'll know why. I still can't get that pecan pie out of my mind.

Saint Joe

Ferguson Country Store, Restaurant and Furniture Workshop
Highway 65 South
(870-439-2234)
Hours: Daily 8:00 A.M.–3:00 P.M. in season; 8:00 A.M.–2:00 P.M. in winter.

Ferguson's was founded in 1973 to display handmade crafts of local artisans. A mile north of the Buffalo National River, its two-story, native-stone-and-wood building is designed in a style popular in the previous century. Today, the store blends into the restaurant, with a shop out back where quality, country-style oak furniture is made. For breakfast, try a homemade cinnamon roll the size of a softball, huge and fluffy buttermilk biscuits with or without sausage gravy, or eggs, pancakes, and other hearty dishes. Lunches range from chicken-fried steak to salads, hamburgers, homemade ham and beans with onions and cornbread, or a chicken-fried chicken sandwich. If you missed the cinnamon roll for breakfast, it's among the lunchtime dessert offerings.

Scott

Cotham's Country Store and Restaurant
Take the England exit off Interstate 440 and follow signs to Scott.
(501-961-9284)
Hours: Tuesday-Friday, 11:00 A.M.–2:00 P.M.; Friday, 5:00 P.M.–8:00 P.M.; Saturday, 11:00 A.M.–8:00 P.M.

Originally opened in 1917 as a general mercantile store, Cotham's has become a place where the elite meet to eat. In the midst of many of the old country-store products and a few new items, politicians, actors, and other celebrities have gathered in the small eating area to gorge

A board listing the day's specials hangs beside a portrait of Bill and Hillary Clinton.

themselves on one of the hubcap hamburgers—they truly are the size of a hubcap—1¼ pound of beef with all the trimmings—or the real fried onion rings. This is one of Bill Clinton's favorite places to eat when he's in town, the waitress said, seating me at the president's table. Maybe it was my imagination, but I felt a surge of power. Or maybe that was after I ate the onion rings.

If you're not in the mood for burgers ($3.97 for regular, $6.63 for hubcap-size), you can order a pork-chop sandwich or the catfish or chicken dinner. Lunch specials such as chicken and dumplings, smothered steak, and pork chops include three vegetables and a drink. For $1.53, you can get a side order of fried green tomatoes that are corn-meal crunchy and tart.

Dessert? Maybe you'd better skip the meal and go straight for the Mississippi Mud Pie, a two-layer chocolate cake with ice cream, hot fudge, and whipped cream. It, too, is about the size of a Mercury Marquis hubcap.

Springdale

Neal's Cafe

806 North Thompson Street
(501-751-9996)
Hours: Monday–Saturday, 6:30 A.M.–7:30 P.M.

You can't miss the hot-pink building of this homey restaurant now in its fifty-fourth year and run by the third and fourth generations of the Neal Family. Popular, you say? The place serves up thirty-thousand pounds of food a week. Everything is made on the spot—no prepackaged mixes here. No boxed instant mashed potatoes, either. They're prepared K.P.-style—peeled by hand before they're boiled and mashed. The menu includes chicken pan-fried in a skillet, roast beef, chicken-fried steak, homemade noodles and dumplings. Pies are made on the spot, too, and are delicious. The cafe's decor includes "old guns and arrowheads my dad found sixty years ago," said owner Don Neal.

West Memphis

Other Voices, Other Tastes

Earl's Hot Biscuits

By Fredric Koeppel

No Natty Bumpo, I get lost every time I drive to West Memphis, Arkansas. So my best recommendation in sending you to Earl's Hot Biscuits is that you get off Interstate 55 somewhere and drive around West Memphis for awhile, getting more and more irritated until your companion suggests stopping to ask directions. You ignore this suggestion, of course, and keep coursing, like a coon dog, in a sort of northerly direction back toward the expressway until you stumble on the service road the famed restaurant fronts and from which it looks out upon the great highway that bisects the southern portion of America.

Those with long memories will recall that Earl's Hot Biscuits, founded in 1945, once graced a corner on Crump Boulevard in Memphis, several tosses of a biscuit from the old bridge. It was an institution distinguished physically for its '40s and '50s decor and a neon sign that featured a jocund and rotund black woman rolling biscuit dough. Flickering neon lights made it seem as if her arms were moving back and forth. That type of sign is a thing of the past, and Earl's today occupies a building far less evocative ("nondescript" is the word).

What remains the same—and this is the reason why Earl's Hot Biscuits should retain an honored place in the culture of the Mid-South—is the quality of the biscuits themselves, which are second to none.

A great biscuit is not a miracle; as with so many wonderful and essential parts of life, a great biscuit is simply a feat of chemistry. Yet craft merging with art is required for estimating the precise amalgam of butter or shortening with flour, salt, baking powder, and soda and milk or buttermilk, and for the restraint required not to mess with the stuff too much. A gentle melding of ingredients, a spare kneading with slightly damp fingertips, an understated rolling out of the dough. Such is the process that results in the meltingly tender, pillowy and crusty conjunction of heat and dough such as Earl's serves, good by itself, with milk gravy, or with honey.

Just as good, however, is the corn muffin, which has about it nothing of the dry crumbling nature of other restaurant corn muffins. This one is plump, moist, grainy, and extremely pure and nutty in flavor, sporting a dark, crusty chapeau. Lunch one day was good but not inspired. Best among our selections were country-fried steak, more substantial and flavorful than most examples, and tasty baked chicken. Mashed potatoes were good, but other vegetables were lackluster. A dish of extremely rich and dense bread pudding revived our regard.

Breakfast, however, was a success in every detail. Grits were neither watery nor gluey, but achieved that perfection of fluffy and grainy texture found in the best-prepared examples. A slab of country ham as deeply flavored as the history of farming in America was bracingly salty—but not over the edge—and set the roofs of our mouths a-tingle. Drenched with red-eye gravy, the combination of grits, ham, and over-easy eggs was heartening and irresistible.

Frederic Koeppel is a food critic for the *Memphis Commercial-Appeal*

Wynne

Kelley's Family Style Restaurant
Highway 64
(870-238-2616)
Hours: Monday-Thursday, 5:30 A.M.–9:00 P.M.; Friday-Sunday, 5:30 A.M.–10:00 P.M.

This is one of two restaurants I visited in Wynne and obviously the more successful one since the dining room is large enough to accommodate a couple of church congregations. Saturday night is the big night for Kelley's. That's when the place is packed for an all-you-can-eat buffet of prime rib, crab legs, shrimp, oysters on the half-shell, and other seafood. Otherwise, the daily lunch buffet draws a good crowd, too. Choices usually include fried chicken, country-fried steak, or another entrée, vegetables, and a salad bar.

Starlite Family Restaurant
369 Highway 64 East
(870-238-8872)
Hours: Monday-Thursday, 6:00 A.M.–10:00 P.M.; Friday and Saturday, open twenty-
    four hours

Agriculture seems to be the dominant business in Wynne. I saw tractor and farm-equipment stores every few miles and vast fields ready for soybeans or cotton or whatever the current cash crop is.

The Starlite is one of two family restaurants in Wynne and is owned by Mary Pretty. Ms. Pretty was not on the premises, so I could not judge if she was named appropriately. The menu was pretty extensive, however. For around seven dollars, you can get all the catfish you can eat. Typical entrées include ham steak, roast beef, smothered steak, and chicken with a choice of vegetables. One of the more unusual items on the menu is a Frito pie, which, according to the waitress, was a kind of Mexican concoction using layers of chili, onions, and cheese topped with

Fritos corn chips. I promised to try one on my next trip, just as soon as my fresh supply of Mylanta arrived.

FLORIDA

Hosford ●   Newport ●
                              ● Perry
        Panacea ● Spring Creek
Port St. Joe ● ● Carrabelle
  Apalachicola
                    ● Cross City
                       ● Chiefland
                                        ● New Smyrna
Cedar Key ●   Beach
  Crystal River ●
     Homosassa ●   ● Orlando
      Brooksville ●
       New Port ●

Apalachicola

Boss Oyster
123 Water Street
(850-653-8612)
Hours: Monday-Saturday, 6:00 P.M.–10:00 P.M.

Some purists—and I admit I'm one of them—like their oysters raw or slightly steamed with melted butter or hot sauce and crackers. No fancy toppings other than a cold beer. Others like to fancy things up a bit and add bacon, cheese, shallots, asparagus, or spinach. If that's your bag, then Boss Oyster is your restaurant. Located on the waterfront, this tin-roofed cafe boasts of providing about any topping you can imagine on its Apalachicola oysters. Sure, you can get them on the half-shell or roasted, but just for fun you may want to try the Oyster Jalapeño (with peppers and Monterey Jack cheese), the Oyster St. George (asparagus, garlic, shallots, and colby cheese), or the Oyster à la Artie (blue crabmeat, artichokes, and Monterey Jack cheese). Don't see anything you like? Create your own topping and your name will be added to the menu.

It would be a shame to go to Boss Oyster and not order oysters, but there are other items on the menu. You can get the Boss Golden Seafood Platter with fried oysters, shrimp, scallops, and fish with fries and slaw for $20.95. This platter would feed a whole crew. Regular oysters are $6.25 a dozen; the fancy-topped ones are around $10.00. My suggestion: Get the three dozen roasted in the shell for $14.25, with an order of onion rings or curly fries and coleslaw.

The Red Top Cafe
Highway 98
(850-653-8612)
Hours: Monday-Saturday, 6:00 A.M.–9:00 P.M.

Besides its excellent breakfasts and meat-and-three lunches, the Red Top's main claim to fame is that country-music hunk Billy Dean once ate here and left them an autographed picture. A small cafe with (of course) a red roof, the Red Top is an all-purpose diner that offers short orders, steaks and chops, and seafood, as well as the daily specials. Maybe because every other restaurant in town serves oysters, the Red Top doesn't have them on the menu. You can get shrimp and grouper and six different kinds of chicken—grilled chicken, fried chicken, smothered chicken, barbecue chicken, Teriyaki chicken, chicken stir-fry—but no oysters. Prices range from $7.99 for the chicken to $13.99 for the grouper and shrimp.

Breakfast is recommended, especially the sausage and biscuits.

Brooksville

Mallie Kyla's Cafe

510 East Liberty Street
(352-796-7174)
Hours: Monday-Friday, 9:00 A.M.–5:00 P.M.; Saturday, 9:00 A.M.–4:00 P.M.

Mallie Kyla's has the distinction of being named one of *Southern Living*'s five Readers' Choice winners in the small-town restaurant category. Much of the credit has to go to the food, which is Southern with some interesting touches, but the ambiance of the restaurant seems to attract customers as well. Brightly colored tablecloths, freshly cut flowers, and the scent of potpourri makes the dining experience delightful. The restaurant, located in the historic Hawkins House, was named after owner Don Hensley's maternal grandmother. "She was an exceptional cook," says Hensley's wife, Larie. "We like to think her spirit is among us as we celebrate life and enjoy a good meal."

Instead of having an extensive menu, the Hensleys have concentrated on a limited but interesting selection. The special of the day when I arrived was meat loaf and scalloped potatoes with a choice of butter-bean soup or clam chowder. By 1:00 P.M., it was gone, gobbled up by a throng of retirees who were in town for a convention. If you miss out on the lunch special, you can always fall back on the salads—white albacore tuna, chicken salad, garden, or Greek—or the sweet Virginia-ham-and-Swiss sandwich on a freshly baked croissant. There is a special dessert for each day, but the oatmeal cake—a scrumptious moist cake with toasted coconut/boiled caramel icing—is available all the time. With a dollop of fresh whipped cream, it is almost sinful.

Carrabelle

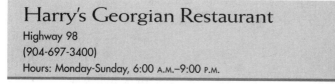

Harry's Georgian Restaurant
Highway 98
(904-697-3400)
Hours: Monday-Sunday, 6:00 A.M.–9:00 P.M.

Located in the heart of Carrabelle, a Gulf Coast town famous for its seafood, Harry's Georgian Restaurant is *the* hangout for local diners. One satisfied customer exiting the restaurant recommended the fried grouper, stopped to remove his toothpick, and added, "But if you don't like grouper, everything else is good, too."

Lunch specials include grouper, of course, but also an assortment of vegetables. The day I stopped, Harry's offered potato salad, corn, green beans, and coleslaw. Oyster stew is on the menu from time to time and is not to be missed. Also recommended is Harry's Crab Casserole from an old family recipe. As expected for a coastal restaurant, you can get almost any kind of fried seafood platter you like, from fried Apalachicola oysters to fried shrimp, fried scallops, or fried grouper.

Another item that's popular is fried Dog Island mullet, which is available, depending on how successful the local fishermen are.

Julia Mae's

Highway 98 in Carrabelle
(850-697-3791)
Hours: Sunday-Thursday, 11:00 A.M.–9:00 P.M.;
  Friday and Saturday, 11:00 A.M.–10:00 P.M.

Julia Mae's lists itself as "world famous," which is kind of a risky label. I once ate at a barbecue joint (I think it was called Big Bubba's) that was world famous, too, but I later learned it was internationally known for having the worst barbecue. Nobody would ever say the food is bad at Julia Mae's. The fried seafood is fresh and the hush puppies are worth seconds. The coleslaw is a little sloppy for my taste, and just looking at the coconut, chocolate, pecan, and Key lime pies adds an inch to your waist. (They make them fresh on Friday, so try to get a slice then). In addition to the fried-seafood platters, Julia Mae's has daily specials of roast beef, hamburger steak, spaghetti, fried chicken, and vegetables. Or you can get a grouper burger or an oyster burger with fries and slaw. And it's a lot better than the barbecue at Big Bubba's.

Other Voices, Other Tastes

By Fred Willard

One of my favorite eateries is Julia Mae's in Carrabelle. They have great fish-camp seafood, cooked broiled or fried, and even better pies. Eat a slice there, then take a whole pie back to your room.

Fred Willard is the author of *Down on Ponce*.

Cedar Key

All during my travels in Florida I had heard about the seafood at Cedar Key, a historic island on the Gulf that once was an important port for shipping cotton and lumber. The town was delightful, a waterfront village of historic wooden and tabby houses that now serve as antique shops and boutiques for tourists. According to a local journalist, it was where naturalist John Muir ended his one-thousand-mile trek. I still had several thousand miles to go on my trek, but I decided to sample the seafood to see if it lived up to its reputation. It did, and it didn't. All the steamed dishes were good, but the fried shrimp and oysters were only marginally better than Long John Silver's. After I had stuffed myself at a couple of the dock restaurants, I discovered that all the locals gathered at a place on the outskirts of town called The Blue Desert Cafe. Now they tell me.

Therese Cavagnaro, The Blue Desert Cafe's owner and chef

The Blue Desert Cafe

12518 Highway 24
(904-543-9111)
Hours: Tuesday-Thursday, 4:00–9:00 P.M.; Friday and Saturday, 4:00–10:00 P.M.

The Blue Desert Cafe doesn't look like much on the outside. Maybe that's because it once was a gas station, grocery store, and bait shop. It's not fancy on the inside, either, unless you count the stuffed coyote on one wall and a poster from the movie *Blue Velvet* on the other. The dining room is about the size of a small living room and has limited seating. There's a bar where you can order just about any brand of beer and a front porch where you can sit and wait the hour or so it usually takes to get seated. You won't find any country-fried steak on the menu, either. About the only things Southern are the Cajun dishes. Owner and chef Therese Cavagnaro cooks pretty much what she likes, and she likes to take the fresh shrimp she buys from the local fishermen and sauté them in garlic with wine, then toss them over a bed of linguine. She cooks other pasta dishes, too, and makes burritos the size of a large sombrero. "I had no idea what I was doing when I opened this place three years ago," says Cavagnaro, a dark curly-haired New Jersey native. "I just wanted to run a restaurant, and I liked to cook. I kept trying new things, and the local folks started coming here. Everything is fresh and made from scratch. That's why it takes so long." And why does she call it the Blue Desert Cafe? "When my partner and I were in town one day, there was a fog rising over the water. It looked like a blue desert." About anything on the menu is recommended, but you can't go wrong with the Cajun Peppered Shrimp and the Garlic Shrimp.

The Brown Pelican

On the dock at Cedar Key
(904-543-5428)
Hours: Monday-Thursday and Sunday, 11:00 A.M.–9:30 P.M; Friday and Saturday,
    11:00 A.M.–10:00 P.M.

While not living up to my expectations, several of the restaurants on the dock at Cedar Key were okay. The fish chowder at The Brown Pelican was nice and spicy, the steamed clams were fresh, and the view of the waterfront as a storm moved in was better than anything I had seen on the Weather Channel. But like any good Southern boy, I had to try the fried shrimp and fried oysters. Not bad—just not memorable. And even with the view, I think I preferred the talkative clientele at The Blue Desert Cafe over the screaming baby that a group of tourists brought in.

Chiefland

Neighbor's Restaurant
U.S. 19, five miles north of Chiefland
(352-493-4724)
Hours: Monday-Saturday, 6:00 A.M.–8:00 P.M; Sunday, 6:00 A.M–3:00 P.M.

Back in the 1930s, Neighbor's Restaurant was a notorious nightclub called The Black Diamond. The original french doors are still there, but little else remains to remind customers of those rowdy days. In addition to the great breakfasts and meat-and-three lunches, the restaurant is best known for a giant fox grapevine out back. It's documented by the University of Florida as the largest in the country. Before you go wandering out to look at the grapevine, however, eat first. The scrambled eggs, corned-beef hash, and biscuits and gravy are quite tasty. And if you're there for lunch, you have a choice of daily specials such as liver and onions, country-fried steak, chicken livers, spaghetti, shrimp, grouper, catfish, clams, fried squash, macaroni and cheese, fried okra, lima beans, or fried corn on the cob.

Cross City

Betty Gassett, owner of Cypress Inn Restaurant

Cypress Inn Restaurant

Highway 19 North
(352-498-7211)
Hours: Monday-Thursday, 5:00 A.M.–9:00 P.M.; Friday and Saturday, 5:00 A.M.–
   10:00 P.M.

Cross City is a lumber town and the men who eat at the Cypress Inn Restaurant have the appetites of lumberjacks. A typical lunch buffet consists of roast beef, roast pork, fried chicken, liver and onions, or country-fried steak, and an assortment of mashed potatoes, squash, fried okra, greens, or other vegetables. On special days, when swamp cabbage is on the menu, the place is even more crowded. Swamp cabbage is the heart of palm that is steamed and is considered a delicacy. Along with the swamp cabbage, the Cypress Inn Restaurant serves fresh mullet, grouper, and catfish. Friday and Saturday nights are steak nights, with the slabs of beef grilled on an open pit with real oak wood.

Crystal River

Front Porch Restaurant and Pie Shop

Highway 19

(352-795-7753)

Hours: Tuesday-Thursday, 7:00 A.M.–8:00 P.M; Saturday, 7:00 A.M.–8:30 P.M.; Sunday,
7:00 A.M.–7:30 P.M.

Stan and Mary Scally and their eight children opened The Front Porch Restaurant and Pie Shop in Dunnellon in 1986 and added the Crystal River location in 1992. Each restaurant is managed by one of their daughters. "Looking back," says Mary Scally, "it's a good thing we didn't know what a full-fledged restaurant was all about, or we probably wouldn't have even attempted it. I can remember opening up, cooking what we thought would be plenty for the day, and be so busy we'd run out of food by 6:00 P.M. with a line waiting to get in." Experience and extra help have made things a little smoother. The restaurant offers daily specials that include chicken and dumplings, fried chicken, fried fish, and an assortment of vegetables, but it is best known for its desserts. *Southern Living* magazine praised the restaurant's pies in one of its issues. Most days you can get apple, cherry, blueberry, pecan, chocolate, peanut butter, coconut cream, banana cream,

Corrie Lovett, granddaughter of Stan and Mary Scally, holds one of the restaurant's strawberry pies.

lemon meringue, Key lime, or strawberry pies. Whole pies range from $7.50 to $10.50 or $1.95 to $2.25 a slice, unless you want ice cream. That's $1.00 extra. As an added attraction, the family performs musical numbers at Christmas and other occasions.

Homosassa

Emily's Family Restaurant
Highway 19 and Cardinal Avenue
(352-628-6559)
Hours: Daily, 6:00 A.M.–8:00 P.M.

Like many of the restaurants in the South, Emily's is owned by a Greek family. George Canaris, whose family also own Debbie's Town House Restaurant in Inverness, Florida, says his grandfather taught his children the secret of running a successful restaurant. He said, "Welcome people as if they are in your home, with good food and conversation and you cannot fail." Canaris adds that he prides himself on running restaurants the old-fashioned way. "Our breakfast potatoes are boiled and hand-grated fresh daily, never frozen or dehydrated. Our eggs and omelettes are pan cooked to order, a superior method to grill cooking. Fresh soups and specials are prepared daily." Well, George seems to be living up to his grandfather's expectations. The breaded pork chop and gravy, with potatoes and peas, was outstanding. Other specials include veal cutlet, country-fried steak, beef liver with grilled onions, fried chicken, and spaghetti. But their specialty is grouper, fried or broiled. Sandwiches and burgers are available, too, and the breakfasts are wonderful, especially the feta-cheese omelette with home fries.

K.C. Crump's Ramshackle Cafe
On the Homosassa River in Homosassa
(352-628-0500)
Hours: Monday–Saturday, 11:00 A.M.–11:00 P.M.; Sunday, 1:00 P.M.–9:00 P.M.

In the early part of the century, the Ramshackle Cafe was a fishing lodge. In 1942, an avid fisherman named Kibbie Charles Crump fell in love with the lodge and persuaded his brother, Stephen Crump, owner of Coca-Cola of Italy, to finance the purchase. Kibbie Crump made the lodge a success because of his hospitality and the serving of fresh vegetables that he grew in his yard and fresh fish caught in the Homosassa River. New owners Stan and Betty Olsen have tried to carry on Crump's tradition, even though it's a little fancier now. Besides the fried-seafood platters and fried-oyster baskets, the restaurant serves an assortment of steaks, salads, and burgers. The soft-shell-crab sandwich on pumpernickel, the fried-grouper sandwich, or the Highway 27 Steakout (sliced beef, onions, mushrooms, and peppers served on a Cuban roll) are all recommended.

K.C. Crump's Ramshackle Cafe

Hosford

Ora's Cafe
Highway 65 North
(850-379-8393)
Hours: Thursday and Friday, 5:00 P.M.–11:00 P.M.; Saturday, 5:30 A.M.–11:00 A.M.
and 5:00 P.M.–9:00 P.M.; Sunday, 11:00 A.M.–3:00 P.M.

Heading north on Highway 65 from Apalachicola through miles and miles of piney woods you don't expect to find many restaurants. I almost sped past Ora's because it looked like a modified house trailer with a wooden sign out front. Inside, the walls are covered with signs on pieces of wood paneling, relics of former owners whose sideline was making signs. Owner Joyce Stephens took over the restaurant in 1996 and has turned it into a place that attracts diners from fifty or sixty miles away. "Everything is fresh," she said. "They say we've got the best mullet around." Ora's is best known for the seafood on Friday and Saturday nights when scallops, shrimp, mullet, crabs, and oysters are on the menu. Sunday lunch features roast beef, pork, hen and dressing, and an assortment of Southern vegetables. My choice is the fried mullet for $7.95, all you can eat. It's fresh, and it's tasty. But so is the coconut pie. Get both.

Port St. Joe

"Gator" in front of Indian Pass Trading Post

Indian Pass Trading Post
Highway C-30 off of Highway 98, between Apalachicola and Port St. Joe
(850-227-1670)
Hours: Sunday-Monday, noon–8:00 P.M.; Friday and Saturday, noon–9:00 P.M.

The Indian Pass Trading Post used to be a country store until James McNeill turned it into the best little oyster bar for miles around. Yes, the Indian Pass oysters are even better than those from Apalachicola. Don't expect anything fancy here. There are a few tables scattered around, but your best bet is to pull up a stool at the bar and order steamed shrimp, steamed oysters, or oysters on the half-shell. You can get a hot dog, hamburger, or fish sandwich, but my suggestion is to simplify. Order a cold beer or soft drink, sit back, and watch Gator slap a lunchroom tray full of oysters or shrimp in the steamer. Randy Branson will shuck your oysters for you, but he won't peel your shrimp. Not even if you beg him. The steamed oysters are not overly large, but they are real delicacies. Dip them in melted butter, take a bite of your saltine cracker, and wash them down with an icy brew. Repeat a couple of dozen times and order the Key lime pie. A dozen oysters is only $4.50.

Newport

Ouzts' Oyster Bar & Canoe Rental
Highway 98
(904-925-6448)
Hours: Monday-Wednesday, 10:00 A.M.–10:00 P.M; Thursday-Saturday, 10:00 A.M.–
    midnight; Sunday, 10:00 A.M.–9:00 P.M.

If you blink when you cross the St. Marks River on Highway 98, you'll miss Newport and Ouzts' Oyster Bar & Canoe Rental. But the town hasn't always been this tiny. At its peak in the nineteenth century it was the fifth largest town in Florida with a flourishing port, a dozen stores, warehouses, wharves, a turpentine distillery, gristmill, and cotton press. Newport and the town of Magnolia, just up the river, attracted not only traders, but visitors as well who came to fish, hunt, and to relax or partake of the cures at the nearby mineral springs. The railroads eventually brought about the demise of Newport and the waterborne cotton trade. Magnolia virtually disappeared and all that remains is a cemetery hidden deep in the woods. Newport became a sleepy community with Ouzts' Oyster Bar as the hub of activity. Canoe renters can paddle seven miles up the pristine St. Marks to Natural Bridge, the site of the last battle of the Civil War. Every March, re-enactors restage the battle. Other attractions nearby are the St. Marks Wildlife Refuge and the St. Marks Lighthouse.

Before and after you head down the river, stop in Ouzts' Oyster Bar and try oysters on the half-shell, steamed oysters, boiled shrimp, bacon-wrapped shrimp, shrimp and rice, shrimp pie, oyster stew, mullet dip, or smoked mullet. A dozen oysters costs $4.95, and everything else is less than $10.00. The bar itself is dark and cozy and just right for unwinding after a canoe trip. Owners Lawana Matthews and Bob Forsythe offer a wide assortment of beers as well as their house special, the Ouzts Shooter, which consists of hot sauce, Tabasco, and horseradish over an oyster, topped off with beer for $2.00. Whew!

New Smyrna Beach

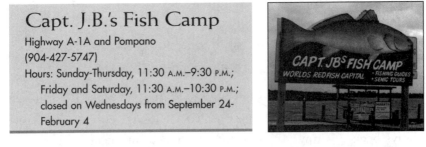

Capt. J.B.'s Fish Camp
Highway A-1A and Pompano
(904-427-5747)
Hours: Sunday-Thursday, 11:30 A.M.–9:30 P.M.;
    Friday and Saturday, 11:30 A.M.–10:30 P.M.;
    closed on Wednesdays from September 24-
    February 4

Capt. J.B.'s Fish Camp is also a bait and tackle shop, so if you're inclined to catch your own dinner, you can get anything you need here. Most of J.B.'s customers prefer their fish already caught, cleaned, and cooked, however. Owner John Bowman was not around when I stopped in, but manager Dennis Okula, a sturdy Irishman, explained that everything on the menu is made from scratch, even the special seasonings. "We have our own crab pots, and we buy our seafood from the local fishermen." J.B. gets his oysters from a private lease, and they are quite tasty. Just about anything on the menu is good. The restaurant was voted one of the top ten in central Florida. The house specialty is the Shipwreck Special—a casserole of shrimp, scallops, and crabmeat served over vegetables and covered with wine-and-cheese sauce. Fried seafood is on the menu, too, including a fried-gator sandwich.

Orlando

Clarkie's Restaurant

3110 South Orange Avenue
(407-859-1690)
Hours: Monday-Friday, 6:00 A.M.–2:00 P.M.; Saturday, 6:00 A.M.–noon; Sunday,
7:00 A.M.–1:00 P.M.

Clarkie's is the sort of place where you're just as likely to sit down beside a corporate executive as a construction worker. At breakfast the morning I was there, a retired factory worker struck up a conversation with a stockbroker about the direction in which the market was heading. The economy looks pretty good, the retiree said, and the stockbroker agreed.

Breakfast at Clarkie's is great if your cholesterol has dipped to a dangerously low level. Sure, you can get the turkey sausage and egg beaters if you're health conscious, but I dug into the farmer's omelette (tomato, potato, onions, ham, and cheese)

*Fran Berkley, owner of
Clarkie's Restaurant*

with a side order of biscuits and gravy and grits. The pancakes looked great, but there's only so much one man can eat. At lunch, you can order sandwiches or burgers off the menu or get one of the daily specials such as country-fried steak or fried fish with a choice of vegetables.

Panacea

Coastal Restaurant

Highway 98
(904-984-2933)
Hours: Thursday-Monday, 6:00 A.M.–10:00 P.M.

If you haven't eaten in several days, the Coastal Restaurant is the place to go. Every day is all-you-can-eat day from a menu that includes a choice of oysters, catfish, mullet, frog legs, and quail. Lunch specials are $3.95 for a meat and two vegetables. Braised beef, yellow rice and chicken wings, chuck-wagon steak, speckled butter beans, fried eggplant, mustard greens, and cucumbers and onions were the daily specials when I stopped in.

Posey's Oyster Bar & Restaurant

End of the St. Marks Trail on the river in Panacea
(850-925-6172)
Hours: Tuesday-Thursday and Sunday, 6:00 A.M.–9:00 P.M.; Friday and Saturday,
6:00 A.M.–10:00 P.M.

Just south of Tallahassee, Posey's Oyster Bar & Restaurant is a ramshackle wood-frame building that offers a back-to-the-basics dining experience. A favorite of locals and tourists alike, Posey's serves some of the freshest Gulf seafood, from oysters on the half-shell (Willie Leverett will shuck oysters for you almost as fast as you can eat them) to baked oysters with a variety of toppings. You can get smoked mullet, a real delicacy, and boiled shrimp. Fried-seafood lovers are in luck, too. Posey's has fried mullet, shrimp, oysters, grouper, and scallops with hush puppies and a choice of potato salad, coleslaw, French fries, or

baked beans. Posey's shows no sign that an interior decorator ever set foot in the place, at least not to decorate. The wooden tables are heavy and plain, and the walls are covered with dollar bills signed by hundreds of customers.

Other Voices, Other Tastes

My-Way Seafood

By Connie May Fowler

Photo by Mike Fowler

Follow Highway 98 through the wisteria-draped pinelands of Florida's Big Bend and eventually you'll roll into the grandly named fishing village of Panacea. Don't drive fast and don't blink. Otherwise, you might whip right past the lavender cinder-block building tucked up under the oaks where Debbie Logan, owner of My-Way Seafood, sells what she proudly calls "the freshest seafood in the world."

This is not about a restaurant, because where seafood is concerned, I prefer to fix my own and to know it was swimming not very long ago.

My-Way is not a restaurant, bar, or trendy cafe. It's a sweetly colored, wide porch with a walk-in refrigerator. It's a speck of Old Florida that stubbornly flourishes despite the "progress" that threatens all around. To seafood lovers, it's what Mecca is to Moslems, an oasis where customers from as far away as Georgia and Alabama make pilgrimages to purchase grouper, snapper, shrimp, mullet, oysters, crab, and other Apalachee Bay and Gulf of Mexico treats, all of which were swimming just hours before.

The establishment's hand-painted roadside sign is graced by a smiling mermaid with the caption, "Come see what kind of fresh seafood the Mermaids have!" Indeed, Logan, who has been a fishmonger since 1984, has made freshness the cornerstone of her business. "It makes you feel good that people who buy from us are putting on the table the best meal for their family. If I can't eat it, I'm not gonna sell it to you," she says with a conviction that would turn even the most jaundiced city-dweller into a believer.

At My-Way you will not find fluorescent-lit display cases, filled with carcasses of days-old unidentifiable fillets. Nope. You step onto the porch, say your hellos, and Logan or one of her sons will ask what they can get for you today.

I've actually heard someone respond, "Do you have any fish?"

"Yes, ma'am! Grouper, mullet, and I think we've got a few snapper left. Come on in and take a look."

The fish are stacked in ice-filled wooden crates and are whole, snout to tail. The shrimp are intact—that is, heads on. Logan insists on selling the whole form, as she calls it, because, "We want you to look at that fish and know what you're getting."

Don't let the intact nature of the seafood put you off. They'll fillet your purchase, no extra charge, and will even include the grouper backs if you're so inclined. If you have no idea what you'd do with a grouper back, suggestions are rendered in mouth-watering detail.

As for shrimp, you'll be asked if you'd like the heads removed. Heads-on shrimp is a local delicacy, but I always opt for removal because I'm perpetually amazed at how quickly the folks at My-Way can pinch off those beady-eyed crustacean brains.

Choosing the right fish can be a daunting task, but My-Way's crew guides even the most novice seafood fan through the process without making anyone feel stupid.

One late winter afternoon as I stood on the porch waiting my turn, a well-appointed woman timidly said, "I need to feed five people. Tonight." She cast a worried glance at a car full of stubborn-faced friends. "And they want fish."

As Logan led the high-heeled woman into the walk-in refrigerator, she recommended grouper because you just can't go wrong with it. Logan then surveyed the fish that her husband had caught earlier that morning and asked, "How about this one?"

"Is it big enough?"

"Oh, yes, ma'am. With a grouper this size, you'll be serving up a gracious plenty."

When Logan says that My-Way offers the freshest seafood in the world, she's not kidding. Every morning, fishermen arrive straight from the docks. If you happen by at the right time, you might meet Mayme Millender. She and her husband, Jessie, have been harvesting shrimp from Carrabelle Bay for over twenty years. With her truck bed loaded with fresh whole shrimp—brownies and hoppers—netted by Jessie, she drives daily into Panacea and sells her bounty to My-Way. If you ask what her preference is regarding shrimp, she'll say, "Hoppers. They're the best tasting."

And if you're foolish enough to ask why they're called hoppers, she'll gladly tell you.

As much as I love My-Way's fresh, high-quality product, I must admit that I love its old Florida atmosphere even more. The oyster shell middens. The bananas with their exotic flowered panicles. The cats who know they've got a good thing going. The wind rustling through the canopy. The unassuming lavender building. The hardworking crew whose honest, no-nonsense approach is both precious and rare. The gossip. The recipes. The locals dispensing hard-won wisdom amid a flurry of tall tales.

When you step onto that porch, hopefully you've left your cell phone in your truck and your worries back at the office. You see, the digital morass of the late-twentieth century doesn't exist here. But be sure to bring your cooler. As the folks at My-Way would say, "You'll want to keep that seafood ice-fresh."

Connie May Fowler is a Florida resident and the author of *Before Women Had Wings*.

Perry

Swain's Family Restaurant
3863 U.S. 19 South
(904-584-5371)
Hours: Monday-Sunday, 7:00 A.M.–9:00 P.M.

Swain's is a spacious, clean restaurant that is short on atmosphere and long on food. You can order most anything off the menu, from burgers and seafood to daily specials such as baked chicken, fried chicken, country steak, or liver and onions. But your best bet is to get the buffet. The country-breakfast buffet is served on Saturdays and Sundays only from 8:00 A.M. to 10:30 A.M., and for about $5.00 you can eat your fill of biscuits and gravy, eggs, bacon, sausage, country ham, and hotcakes. The lunch buffet is $5.99, evening buffet is $6.99, Sunday buffet is $7.99, and the seafood buffet on Friday and Saturday evenings from 5:00 to 9:00 P.M. is $12.99.

Spring Creek

Spring Creek Restaurant
365 Spring Creek Road (about twenty miles south of Tallahassee)
(850-926-3751)
Hours: Wednesday-Friday, 5:00 P.M.–10:00 P.M.; Saturday and Sunday, noon–
10:00 P.M.

By Eileen M. Drennan

Nestled under a grove of live oaks at the end of a dirt road, the Spring Creek restaurant is a small family-run shrine to fresh, local seafood. "If we can't get it fresh," says owner Leo Lovel of his North Florida landmark, "we don't serve it."

For twenty years, they've been getting it fresh for hungry souls who think nothing of driving twenty or thirty miles for the mondo Mate's Platter ($14.95 for shrimp, oysters, mullet, and deviled crab), grouper, stone-crab claws, or bacon-wrapped shrimp. Leo, who raises soft-shell crabs out back with his son, Ben, figures each week he goes through 250 pounds of mullet, 200 pounds of grouper, 150 pounds of shrimp, and 150 pounds of assorted other fish.

Though seafood is the real catch here, steak, hamburger, and fried chicken are served, too. (And don't forget to ask for the cheese grits). The Spring Creek salad is really a mini-salad bar at your table. The iceberg lettuce wedges, cherry tomatoes, green onions, and cucumbers are served in a large wooden bowl. Mason jars of croutons and bacon bits are at every table, as are wine bottles of the house dressing, a Ranch style that Lovel's mother invented.

Do save room for dessert. The cloudlike pies—chocolate peanut butter, Key lime, and coconut cream—are to die for. If you feel generous, save a piece of fish for the stray cats who panhandle out front. They may be skittish, but they are always grateful for the kindness of strangers.

—*Eileen M. Drennan is a reporter for the* Atlanta Journal-Constitution.

GEORGIA

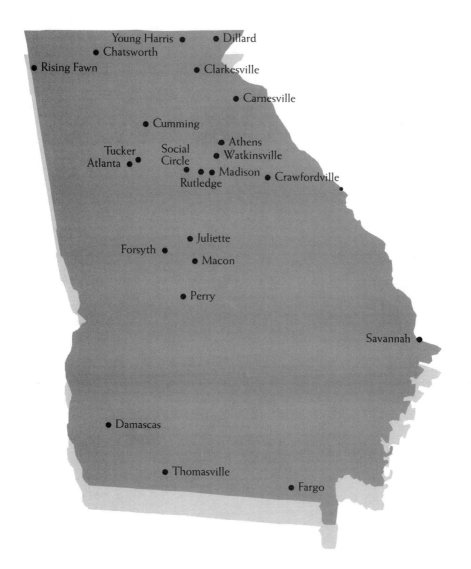

Young Harris ●   ● Dillard
● Chatsworth
● Rising Fawn   ● Clarkesville

● Carnesville

● Cumming

Athens ●
Tucker   Social   ● Watkinsville
Atlanta ●●   Circle
● ● Madison   ● Crawfordville
Rutledge

● Juliette
Forsyth ●   ● Macon

● Perry

Savannah ●

● Damascas

● Thomasville
● Fargo

Athens

Charlie Williams' Pinecrest Lodge
Off Whitehall Road (follow the signs)
(706-353-2606; 800-551-4267)
Hours: Friday and Saturday, 5:00 P.M.–10:00 P.M.; Sunday, noon–4:00 P.M.

Folks around the Athens area have been eating at Charlie Williams's for more than sixty years. In the beginning, Williams cooked for just friends, after working all day at a local wholesale food firm. But as more people sought him out for his legendary barbecue, Williams hauled rock from surrounding fields and built the Milam Room at the Pinecrest Lodge to seat fifty to seventy-five people. Two years later, he added the Stone Room and seating for two hundred and fifty. Thirty-two years later, the Delwood Room with a seating capacity of three hundred and fifty was added, along with a small, operating water wheel. Charlie's nephew, Mike Williams, took over operations in 1976 and enclosed the Stone Room's porch with big picture windows to create a year-round dining area for another one hundred. And still they kept coming. Another section, the Wheel Room, was added in 1989 for one hundred twenty-five additional seats and access for the handicapped.

Why do so many people come to the Pinecrest Lodge? Well, it's an interesting place with a sharecropper's cabin, a blacksmith's shop, a re-constructed moonshine still, and a forty-foot water wheel. But those are just attractions for an after-dinner walk. Inside this hodge-podge of a lodge is one of the largest and best buffets you will find—sixty or more items. A Sunday buffet with catfish and fried chicken is served for under $10.00, but most folks come for the night meal when, for $16.95, you can get all of the fried shrimp, oysters, catfish, sirloin steak, clams, baked chicken, barbecue pork, barbecue ribs, Brunswick stew, clam chowder, vegetables, and salad you can eat. Sometimes there are quail and crab legs, too. You can fill up on boiled shrimp, crab, and salad, but the best food on the bar is fried.

Atlanta

Bobby and June's Kountry Kitchen
375 Fourteenth Street
(404-876-3872)
Hours: Monday-Friday, 6:00 A.M.–8:00 P.M.; Saturday, 6:00 A.M.–2:00 P.M.

Bobby and June's is only a few blocks from the skyscrapers of downtown Atlanta, but you will think you're miles away in the country once you climb the steps to the rustic cabin's front porch and sit for a spell in one of the rocking chairs. Or maybe you want to save your sitting for after you stuff yourself with barbecue, Brunswick stew, or one of the daily meat-and-three specials such as fried chicken, steak and gravy, macaroni and cheese, pickled beets, fried okra, creamed potatoes, turnip greens, or coleslaw. A lunch special costs less than $7.00 for the meat-and-three, or you can get a three-vegetable plate for $4.59. A bowl of Brunswick stew will run you another $2.10. If you can't make it for lunch, I recommend breakfast. Bobby and June's biscuits are wonderful, especially if you slice them open and slather on some butter and jelly or a slice of fried streak-o-lean.

The Colonnade

1879 Cheshire Bridge Road N.E.

(404-874-5642)

Hours: Monday-Friday, 11:00 A.M.–2:30 P.M. and 5:00 P.M.–9:00 P.M.; Saturday,
11:00 A.M.–2:30 P.M. and 5:00 P.M.–10:00 P.M.; Sunday, 11:00 A.M.–9:00 P.M.

By Nancy Roquemore

To say that Atlanta's Colonnade Restaurant is just a meat-and-three would be a serious understatement. With as many as fifty entrées on the menu and more than twenty-five side-dish, salad, and vegetable choices, the 'Nade, as it is affectionately called, has one of the most complete menus in town.

But when it comes to atmosphere and attitude, the Colonnade easily fits into the down-home style of a meat-and-three. As one of Atlanta's oldest establishments (according to our calculations, seventy-five years or more), the restaurant tends to operate like an old Southern lady— genteel, polite, and comforting.

The comfort comes from the food, mostly dishes like your mama made, that is, if you were raised in the "real" South: black-eyed peas, fresh stewed corn, fried okra, butter beans, and sliced tomatoes. Then there are the salads that used to be found only in tearooms of the '40s and '50s: tomato aspic, congealed bing cherry, and pear-and-cheese.

Everyday entrées include some of the best Southern fried chicken in town, lamb chops and shanks, turkey and celery dressing, the best fried shrimp, oysters, and scallops off the Georgia coast, grilled pork chops, fried catfish (whole or filleted), trout (fried, grilled or stuffed), salmon croquettes, country-ham steak with red-eye gravy and grits and, probably the bestseller, chicken pot pie.

Don't stop there, though. The Colonnade has some of the best beef in town: prime rib, T-bone, rib-eye, and fillet. Then there are the blackboard specials that include exotics (at least to a lot of the restaurant's clientele) such as grouper, mahi-mahi, sockeye salmon, frog legs, and soft-shell crab. Prices range from about $7.00 for a meat and two vegetables and bread to $15.95 for some of the seafood items.

Ask a regular or even a first-time patron and they will proclaim the

Rhea Anna Merritt serves customers at The Colonade.

Colonnade's breads the best in the world: yeast rolls that melt in your mouth and tiny cornbread muffins. Desserts range from coconunt, banana, or chocolate cream pie to fresh cobblers and strawberry shortcake.

The customers are a mix of "old Atlanta," new urbanites, families, politicians, and regular out-of-towners. Because the restaurant is located on the property of the Cheshire Motor Inn, where a lot of trade-show visitors and antique dealers stay when they're in town, the cast of characters reminds you of a traveling show that comes to town every month.

A few of the waitresses have been at the Colonnade for more than thirty years, and even though they no longer sport beehive hairdos and blue eye shadow, they still freely dispense "honeys" and "dahlin's" to the customers. Owners Paul and Christ Jones are natives of Michigan, but the restaurant's menu and kitchen staff have remained basically the same as it was when they took over almost twenty years ago. They recognize the value of the axiom that if it ain't broke, don't fix it.

—*Nancy Roquemore is a freelance food editor in Atlanta.*

Mary Mac's Tea Room

224 Ponce de Leon Avenue
(404-876-6604)
Hours: Monday-Friday, 11:00 A.M.–4:00 P.M. and 5:00 P.M.–8:00 P.M.

Just because you drove all the way from Walhalla, South Carolina, to Atlanta doesn't mean you're obliged to eat every meal at one of the fancy Buckhead restaurants. There's nothing wrong with sampling the crab cakes at the Atlanta Fish Market or the Georgia mountain trout at the Horseradish Grill, but save a couple of lunch dates for some of the city's true Southern restaurants.

Mary Mac's Tea Room is not fancy. As my dear departed friend (newspaper columnist) Lewis Grizzard used to say, "There ain't no put-on to them." Mary Mac's is an Atlanta institution known for good, plain Southern meats and vegetables in generous quantities.

Diners are given pencils to write their orders chosen from a menu crowded with selections ranging from creamed corn to collard greens.

Other Voices, Other Tastes

By Calvin Trillin

I haven't been to the South in awhile, but when I was there I used to eat at a place called Mary Mac's that had wonderful "potlikker." I liked Brunswick stew a lot, too, which is hard to get anywhere outside of the South.

As for grits, I always say that people started eating them when Jimmy Carter was in office and that some of them actually have two-thirds of that same box of grits left. I tell people it can be used in anything that calls for wall spackle.

Calvin Trillin is a *New Yorker* contributor and author of *Alice, Let's Eat* and other books.

Adventuresome Yankees are urged to try the "pot likker" and corn bread. No, pot likker is not some new street drug; it's the delicious broth that's left when you cook the greens, preferably with a piece of fatback or streak-o-lean for seasoning. A word of advice: If you're dining with a group, be sure and grab the cinnamon rolls as soon as the bread basket is placed on the table. They go fast. Prices are in the five-dollars-and-up range, depending on the entrée and number of vegetables.

Photo by Jean Shiffrin
Sammie Carson serves up a plate at Son's Place.

Son's Place
100 Hurt Street
(404-581-0530)
Hours: Monday-Friday, 7:00 A.M.–
4:00 P.M.

One of finest soul-food places in town used to be Deacon Burton's. Alas, the Deacon died, and there was a family squabble over who would take over the legendary restaurant. Efforts to keep Deacon's going were less than successful, so Lenn Storey, a scion of the soul-food king, opened his own restaurant. Son's Place has a brighter decor than the old Deacon's with its wobbly tables and mismatched chairs. Son's tables are covered with yellow-checkered, plastic tablecloths with vases of fresh flowers, and the steam table is overflowing with crispy fried chicken, chicken livers, chicken pot pie, and an assortment of fresh vegetables. There's no fancy china here, just compartmentalized plastic trays reminiscent of grammar school, the army, or prison, depending on which career path you took. Whatever you get, fill one of those little compartments with collard greens and another with a couple of fried, flat cornmeal hoecakes. Cobblers are always on the menu and the lemon cheesecake and pound cake are worth taking home for later. Prices range from three to four dollars for breakfast to five to six dollars for a meat and two vegetables for lunch.

Thelma's Kitchen
768 Marietta Street
(404-688-5855)
Hours: Monday-Friday, 7:30 A.M.–4:30 P.M.; Saturday, 7:30 A.M.–2:30 P.M.

Before the Olympics hit town, Thelma's had a thriving lunch business just a couple of blocks from the heart of downtown. But, with the construction of Centennial Park, Thelma Grundy had to relocate several blocks away at a more inconvenient address. The new building is brighter and less cramped than the old quarters, and the food is just as good. A former practical nurse, Grundy cooks the kind of food her mother prepared in rural Georgia. "I used to try different things," she says. "I'd put a sample in the stove to see how it would turn out. If it wasn't any good, I'd try something different." In addition to Southern breakfasts with country ham, bacon, sausage, and fried salmon patties, Grundy serves meat-and-two or meat-and-three lunches cafeteria style. Daily specials include fried chicken, country-fried steak, ribs, beef liver, chicken liver, baked ham, pork chops, and hot dogs. Prices range from around $5.00 to $7.50. The cobblers and pies are always good.

Carnesville

Red Minnow Fish Lodge
Highway 106, three miles south of Carnesville
(706-245-5105)
Hours: Friday and Saturday, 5:00 P.M.–10:00 P.M.; Sunday, noon–4:00 P.M.

The Red Minnow Fish Lodge adds new meaning to the term backroad buffet. Set out in the woods on a small stream, the Red Minnow is a rustic wooden building that has several large rooms, jammed with long tables and folding metal chairs. Don't look for Martha Stewart decorating touches here, just plenty of good fried seafood, catfish, boiled shrimp, Brunswick stew, barbecue pork, steamed crab legs, onion rings, French fries, coleslaw, and tasty hush puppies. Prices are twelve dollars for all-you-care-to-eat, plus two dollars a pound for crab legs. My recommendation is to order fried oysters and plenty of them. They are lightly battered and fried just enough to still be juicy. With the exception of the catfish and the crab legs, the rest of the menu is average.

Chatsworth

Edna's
Highway 411 South
(706-695-4968)
Hours: Tuesday-Saturday, 11:00 A.M.–7:45 P.M.

Chatsworth is at the foot of Fort Mountain, so named because of a mysterious, centuries-old stone formation at its peak. But there's no mystery about the popularity of Edna Blackwell's restaurant.

Honest home-cooking brings in the crowds to feast on fried chicken, meat loaf, fresh vegetables, definitive corn muffins, and homemade desserts. Edna's business card features a chicken in a chef's hat and the motto: "Our chicken dinners are worth crowing about," and that's what everybody around Fort Mountain has been doing for years. Prices are in the five-to-six-dollar range for meat-and-three lunches.

Clarkesville

LaPrade's

Highway 197, north from Clarkesville
(706-947-3313)
Hours: Thursday-Sunday, breakfast is served from 8:00 A.M.–9:00 A.M.; lunch from
12:30 P.M.–2:00 P.M.; dinner from 7:00 P.M.–8:00 P.M.

LaPrade's is an all-purpose tourist stop on Lake Burton in north Georgia, a few miles from the Appalachian Trail. In 1916, John LaPrade built a camp on six hundred acres to feed and house the engineers and workers when Georgia Power began damming the Tallullah River to create Lake Burton. Since 1925, LaPrade's has been a rustic mountain resort that offers overnight stays in cabins, boat rentals at the marina, and some of the best fried chicken you'll find anywhere. Meals are served family style with hot biscuits, cornbread, fresh vegetables from the LaPrade garden, coleslaw, desserts, and drinks. The fried chicken—crispy gold on the outside, juicy on the inside and seasoned just right—is served at dinner for $11.75. Lunch ($8.75) is chicken and dumplings plus pork roast, country steak or another meat-of-the-day, vegetables, and cobbler. All of these meals are good, but there's something special about eating a breakfast ($6.75) of country ham, sausage, red-eye gravy, grits, scrambled eggs, biscuits, and sorghum syrup on a chilly morning when the fog is still hovering over the lake.

Crawfordville

Southern Magnolia Restaurant

131 Broad Street
(706-456-3333)
Hours: Monday-Thursday, 11:00 A.M.–8:00 P.M.; Friday and Saturday, 11:00 A.M.–
   9:00 P.M.; Sunday, 11:00 A.M.–4:00 P.M.

For years, Mrs. Bonner's Cafe was an institution in Crawfordville. Stories about her legendary sweet-potato pie were passed down from generation to generation. Imagine my disappointment, then, when I went to the plain storefront restaurant on the square and found it was closed. A clerk at the courthouse said Mrs. Bonner was in a nursing home but that a new restaurant had opened down the street. "It's pretty good," she said. Well, it was lunchtime and I was hungry, Mrs. Bonner's or no Mrs. Bonner's.

The Southern Magnolia was a pleasant surprise. It is far fancier than Mrs. Bonner's with a mural along the length of one wall that depicts a Southern scene with a plantation house and a smaller cottage. "The small one is my house," said owner Ruth Easters, who added that her daughter, Jan Easters Cumber, was the artist. The Easters—Ruth and husband Cy—opened the restaurant in January 1998, after retiring to the area from Stone Mountain. And, to assure themselves of success, they hired the lady who had cooked for Mrs. Bonner for twenty-some years. "We added a few new things," Ruth said, "but everybody had gotten used to certain dishes, so we still serve those. Everybody loves our fried chicken and fried green tomatoes."

I had to agree with her that the fried chicken and tomatoes were first-rate. So were the macaroni and cheese and the butter peas. Other daily specials include country steak, liver and onions, meat loaf, baked chicken, and salmon patties. Sunday dinner features roast beef, ham, fried chicken, and turkey and dressing. The plate lunch specials are $5.95, but you can also order from a menu that has been expanded from Mrs. Bonner's. One of the specialties of the house is the Magnolia onion, a whole onion fried to a delicate crispness with a tangy dip. Steaks, catfish, flounder, and fried shrimp are also available with an all-you-can-eat salad bar. And, yes, you can still get the same kind of sweet-potato pie that Mrs. Bonner's served.

Cumming

The Lantern Inn
Georgia Highway 369
(770-887-3080)
Hours: Friday, 5:00 P.M.–11:00 P.M.; Saturday, 6:00 A.M.–11:00 P.M.

Mike Jones as Elvis

Well, maybe Elvis hasn't left the building after all. He reappears every weekend in a Forsyth County restaurant/club north of Atlanta in the form of Mike Jones— garbage collector by day, Elvis impersonator by night. Before the ten o'clock show on Fridays and Saturdays, Jones does double duty in the kitchen, frying up catfish and chicken for the country buffet. And on Saturdays, he's up at 5:00 A.M., baking biscuits and cooking breakfast. "My daddy told me if I stuck with him, I'd be rolling in the dough," Jones quips during his act. "But all I do is roll out the dough."

Dressed in black leather for the early show, Jones works the crowd, singing and handing out polyester scarves while his father, Harold, operates the karaoke machine. The crowd,

(Left to right) Virginia, Mike, and Harold Jones of The Lantern Inn

mostly boisterous locals, sends up requests on slips of paper. "Here's one," Jones says. "Get back in the kitchen. We're out of catfish."

Between acts, his sister, Debbie, performs as Patsy Cline and various members of the audience sing, too. Jones's mother, Virginia, keeps tabs on the buffet table and makes sure everyone has iced tea or a long-necked beverage to drink.

Then it's Elvis again in his white sequined jump suit and cape in a low-budget version of the King's Vegas act. "I can cook a hunka, hunka burning catfish," he croons, and he's right. The catfish and chicken are deep-fried golden brown and accompanied with a salad bar and delicious homemade potato salad. But the food is incidental at the Lantern Inn. Go for the show. Jones does a not-too-bad job imitating Elvis and best of all, he doesn't take himself seriously.

Damascus

Other Voices, Other Tastes

The Power Line

By Robert Coram

The Power Line Restaurant in Damascus sits in the middle of a seventy-acre cotton field under the biggest set of power lines you ever saw. Steel towers stand directly behind and in front of the restaurant; towers with horizontal members that support layers and layers of high-tension wires. As you walk from your car across the dusty parking lot, you hear the wires humming and sizzling.

It might be the only restaurant in the South that has its own buzz going.

The tin-roofed cypress building has heart-pine

floors and walls and seats two hundred and fifty. From Wednesday through Saturday it offers up food that draws people from all around southwest Georgia, eastern Alabama, and the Florida panhandle. During hunting season when the local hunting lodges are filled with shooters from all over the country, dozens of men in cammies come trooping into the restaurant each evening about 9 P.M. ready to chow down on seafood and steaks.

The occasional entertainment is reliant on karaoke singers. "We are after a relaxed kind of supper-club atmosphere," says owner Owen Tabb.

One unusual thing about this restaurant is that in a land where seafood is deep-fried, and steaks are treated like burnt offerings, you can get grouper and red snapper broiled or grilled, and a sixteen-ounce Power Line Cut rib-eye that the menu says should not be ordered well-done.

And while they throw too much lemon pepper and cajun spice atop the grilled fish, the cooks know to remove it from the grill while it is still moist.

Appetizers include an onion bloom, fried mushrooms, cheese sticks, and buffalo wings. The twelve-ounce prime rib and the sixteen-ounce rib-eye are the most expensive items on the menu—$13.95.

The Power Line is on Highway 45, one mile north of Damascus, eight miles south of Arlington. Look for the big wooden sign on the east side of the road. Go down the dirt road one mile, and there it is. Telephone: (912-725-4138). Hours: Wednesday-Saturday, 5:00 P.M–10:00 P.M.

—Robert Coram, an Atlanta writer, is the author of *Narcs* and *Atlanta Heat*.

Dillard

Dillard House

Off U.S. 441, just north of Dillard and Clayton and about two miles from the North
  Carolina border
(800-541-0671 or 706-746-5348)
Hours: Monday-Sunday, breakfast is served from 7:00 A.M.–10:00 P.M.; lunch from
  11:30 P.M.–5:00 P.M.; and dinner from 5:00 P.M.–8:30 P.M.

The Dillard House is a legend in north Georgia and even in neigh-
boring states. The restaurant and motel are located in a picture-postcard
setting in the foothills of the Blue Ridge Mountains with a fantastic view.

If you're planning to visit the Dillard House, it's best not to eat for
three or four days beforehand. The meals are served family style, which
means they bring out bowls and platters of food and set them on the
wooden tables, just like your Mama did. The meal includes three meat
entrées and at least seven vegetables, most of which are grown by the
Dillards. This is not counting the coleslaw and Calico Salad (pickled
tomatoes and cucumbers) for appetizers. Usually you can count on having fried chicken and country ham for lunch with another meat entrée
such as pork cutlets, country steak, prime rib, or whatever else the cooks
are in the mood to prepare added for dinner.

Since it's all you can eat, they keep bringing out more food until you
collapse from exhaustion. And then there's cobbler and ice cream for
dessert and an assortment of the Dillard House's own apple or peach
butter, blackberry jelly or other preserves with the homemade rolls. Lunch
and dinner are $13.95.

Breakfast is another matter. For $10.95, you can get country ham, sau-
sage patties, link sausage, bacon, pork tenderloin, scrambled eggs, country-fried potatoes, grits, sausage gravy, red-eye gravy, stewed apples,
cinnamon rolls, biscuits, blueberry muffins, fresh fruit, and fresh juice.
I'm not talking about a choice of these; you can eat ALL of these things
if you're so inclined.

If you're too stuffed to travel any farther, the Dillard House has cottages with tennis courts, a children's petting zoo, and horseback riding. You can hike on the many trails in the area or go whitewater rafting on the nearby Chattooga River of *Deliverance* fame.

Fargo

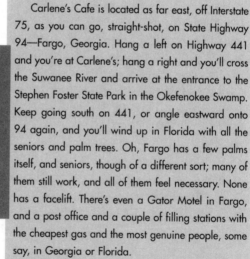

Other Voices, Other Tastes
Carlene's Cafe
By Janice Daugharty

Carlene's Cafe is located as far east, off Interstate 75, as you can go, straight-shot, on State Highway 94—Fargo, Georgia. Hang a left on Highway 441 and you're at Carlene's; hang a right and you'll cross the Suwanee River and arrive at the entrance to the Stephen Foster State Park in the Okefenokee Swamp. Keep going south on 441, or angle eastward onto 94 again, and you'll wind up in Florida with all the seniors and palm trees. Oh, Fargo has a few palms itself, and seniors, though of a different sort; many of them still work, and all of them feel necessary. None has a facelift. There's even a Gator Motel in Fargo, and a post office and a couple of filling stations with the cheapest gas and the most genuine people, some say, in Georgia or Florida.

According to Doris Long, current owner of Carlene's Cafe, over a span of some sixty-odd years, numerous area people have owned the old street-front cafe, beginning with Artic Griffis Brooks.

Aside from the all-you-can-eat buffet, featuring fried chicken and hopping John (you don't have to mix your rice and peas) and the tenderest cornbread in southeast Georgia (Ruthie, cook and waitress, even taught me how to make it), what I like about Carlene's is watching the customers: locals drifting in from the deer woods, the logging woods, and the old homeplaces scattered throughout the Clinch and Echols County flatwoods. My home, Echols County, stops just west of the Fargo city limits, at Suwanoochee Creek. I like the contrast of the natives with the foreigners come to scout out the Okefenokee. The natives already know the Okefenokee, heart of their homeland; like their parents and grandparents, dipping back into the generations, they work and live there. The foreigners . . . well, they can't quite get over these down-to-earth Fargoians with all the time in the world to sit and eat and swap news in an atmosphere of Indian artifacts and crochet-work by the good ladies of Fargo trying to make an extra dime or just sharing with the world something pretty they've made.

Table one, on the right side of the single-room, wood-paneled cafe is reserved for the regulars—no sign, the reservation is simply understood—honest, hard-working men in for the noon meal we call dinner. Or you can breakfast at 5 A.M. and stay for supper—you have to leave by 8 P.M. unless you aren't quite through eating.

Friday, fish day, marks the end of the work week and the start of the weekend: more young people on Saturdays, and on Sundays, the same crowd but dressed up after church. Any day of the week, while you eat, Ruby and Carlene wander from table one to table ten with pitchers of sweet, steeped tea. They'll get you unsweet tea—no problem, ma'am—if that's what you want.

One fellow, at table one, who is thin as a sunset shadow of a pine, doesn't eat his chicken fried or his green beans seasoned with smoked pork. So every day, Monday through Sunday, exactly at 12 o'clock noon, as signaled by the next-door Methodist Church chimes, pealing off old-timey hymns, his plate of boiled food is waiting. There are bottles of pepper sauce on the tables for your greens, and you can visit the sparkling chrome-and-white kitchen if you have time. And if you want to pick your teeth, that's okay, too. Everybody else does.

Janice Daugharty, a native of Echols County, Georgia, is the author of *Whistle* and other novels.

Forsyth

The Farm House Restaurant
22 West Main Street
(912-994-2165)
Hours: Monday–Saturday, 7:00 A.M.–9:00 P.M.; Sunday, 7:00 A.M.–2:00 P.M.

By Kent Mitchell

To thousands, Forsyth is a stopping point halfway between their northern hometown and their Florida destination. That must be why there are so many motels and fast-food joints at Exit 62 on Interstate 75 because there's no other draw to make people get off the interstate. The only other things are a college campus that's for sale (former Bessie Tift College), the Georgia Public Safety Training Center, and an old mill converted into a flea market and furniture outlet.

All those travelers suffering from indigestion after greasy fries and burgers only had to drive about two blocks beyond Wendy's to find the Monroe County courthouse. Two right turns later, they would have landed in front of the Forsyth Square Bed and Breakfast and the Farm House Restaurant. Both are owned and run by Jack and Shirley Spillers for the last fourteen years.

Food is served buffet style, but it's unusual in that the Spillers serve *fresh* Southern-style vegetables such as made-from-scratch rutabagas, turnip greens, sweet-potato soufflé, cornbread (not the sweet kind), biscuits, great fried chicken, ham pot pie to die for, and top-of-the-line fried green tomatoes. Buffet prices are $4.50 for one serving of meat, two vegetables, bread, and butter. Or you can get extra fried green tomatoes at thirty-five cents a slice.

Breakfast is worth getting up early for, too, even if you aren't staying at the Forsyth Square Inn. The country-ham breakfast with two eggs, biscuits, and grits is only $4.50. Or, if your cholesterol is dangerously low, get the Farm House milk gravy over two biscuits with two pieces of streak-o-lean for $1.95.

—Kent Mitchell is a reporter for the Atlanta Journal-Constitution

Juliette

Whistle Stop Cafe

Downtown Juliette (Take Exit 61 off Interstate 75 and go east eight miles.)
(912-994-3670)
Hours: Monday-Saturday, 8:00 A.M.–2:00 P.M.; Sunday, noon–5:00 P.M.

Anybody who saw the movie, *Fried Green Tomatoes*, or read Fanny Flagg's novel, knows about the cafe near the railroad tracks. For filming purposes, the Hollywood folks used an old general store in Juliette as a cafe. It seemed like such a good idea that Robert Williams and Jerie Lynn Williams decided to open a real cafe in the building after the actors left. The rest of the town has become something of a tourist attraction as well, drawing visitors to nearby Jarrell Plantation and to the antique and gift shops. The restaurant itself is usually packed on weekends with folks wistful for a glimpse of small-town life from the past and for a taste of Southern cooking. Fried green tomatoes are the specialty, of course, and every meal comes with one slice. If you want more, you can get a side order for $2.55. Other choices include barbecue ribs, meat loaf, fried chicken, collard greens, cabbage, rutabagas, baked beans, or baked potato. Prices range from $2.50 for breakfast to $6.95 for a meat, three vegetables, dessert, and a beverage for lunch. While you're in the area, you may want to take a tour of the 1847 plantation house at Jarrell Plantation. Annual events include a July 4th celebration, sheepshearing, spinning and weaving demonstrations, syrup making, and candlelight Christmas tours. For information about these events, call 912-986-5172.

Macon

Photo by Jonee Ansa

Other Voices, Other Tastes
Nu-Way

By Tina McElroy Ansa

Listen, I don't want to hear anything about grease and fat and cholesterol and gas and heartburn and artificial coloring and such. All I want to hear is, "What you gon' have, Sugar?" Because Nu-Way hot dogs and hamburgers have been feeding my soul in my hometown of Macon, Georgia, for as long as I can remember. Sitting in a beauty shop waiting to get my hair done on a Saturday in the 1950s, someone would come in with a black-and-white paper bag stained greasy with hot dogs and hamburgers for the shop. On the way home from a James Brown concert at the Macon auditorium in the '60s, it seemed a natural thing to swing by the Nu-Way across the street to get a fountain Coke and a couple of hamburgers. You always needed more than one. Not because they were small like Krystals and mostly bun, but because you always wanted another one.

Even in segregated Macon, Nu-Way was an inviting place. Most of the waitresses and cooks behind the counter were black, as I was. And they all seemed to know and like me. The space was hardly big enough for a restaurant; too small and close to want to sit down anyway. Just big enough to stand, get your order in a greasy bag and move on to a pleasant place to eat.

Tina McElroy Ansa, author of *Ugly Ways* and *Baby of the Family*, lives on St. Simons Island, Georgia.

Madison

Ye Olde Colonial Restaurant

108 East Washington Street
(706-342-2211)
Hours: Monday-Saturday, 5:30 A.M.–8:30 P.M. Closed on major holidays.

Usually it's wise to stay away from any restaurant with "Ye Olde" in its name, but not in this case. Popular with locals and tourists alike, Ye Olde Colonial Restaurant offers cafeteria-style breakfasts, lunches, and dinners in what used to be a bank on the public square in historic Madison. Owner Jim Cunningham says he tries to use locally grown fruits and vegetables whenever possible. "We have vine-ripe tomatoes that we buy from a farmer in Rutledge," Cunningham says, "and we usually get all the squash we can handle in season. One of our most popular dishes is blackberry cobbler. Folks can't get enough of that." Among the vegetables, squash casserole and sweet potatoes are local favorites. A typical menu includes roast beef, country-fried steak, and fried chicken. Several times a week Cunningham cooks barbecue pork with a North Carolina vinegar-based sauce or barbecue beef with a sweeter tomato-based sauce. Prices range from $2.39 to $3.49 for entrées and about $1.00 each for vegetables. Cobblers are $1.25. And while you're in Madison, check with the Chamber of Commerce on the square for a guide to many of the antebellum homes in town.

Perry

New Perry Hotel

800 Main Street

(912-987-1000)

Hours: Monday-Sunday, 7:00 A.M.–10:00 P.M. for breakfast; 11:30 A.M.–2:30 P.M for lunch.; 5:30 P.M.–9:00 P.M.

The New Perry Hotel was built in 1925 on the site of the original Perry Hotel, an establishment that had served as lodging for passengers and workers on the stagecoach line and the railroad. With the construction of U.S. Highway 41 from Tennessee to Florida in the 1920s, the New Perry became a popular stop for tourists. Nowadays, if you're driving on Interstate 75, it's a little harder to get to the New Perry, but thousands still make the effort. Owners Yates and Harold Green say that more than eighty percent of the diners have eaten at the hotel before. Most say they come back because they like the familiarity of the atmosphere and the food. And it is good Southern comfort food like fried chicken, chicken and dumplings, homemade tomato-and-rice soup served with oyster crackers, rolls, and cornbread sticks. Some of the vegetables tasted a little bland the day I was there—particularly the cabbage and shredded yams—but the chicken and dumplings were delicious. So was the Southern pecan pie. I recommend it. Lunch prices are around seven dollars for meat, two vegetables, soup, and bread.

Rising Fawn

Rising Fawn Cafe
Exit 1 off Interstate 59 near the Tennessee-Alabama line
(706-462-2277)
Hours: Monday-Sunday, 7:00 A.M.–9:00 P.M.

Anybody who doesn't stop at a place called the Rising Fawn Cafe has no romance in his or her soul. Rising Fawn has a Native American ori-gin, of course. American Indians were po-etic in the names they chose for places, unlike developers these days who label sub-divisions Hidden Acres and Brandywine Hills. A rustic, unpainted wooden building with an adjoining antique shop, The Rising Fawn Cafe is located on a hill just behind an enormous truck stop. Owner Gene Wallin, who was partaking of a plate of bar-becue pork and collards, complained that the previous truck stop had burned and the new owners had erected a ten-foot chain-link fence to discourage truckers from eat-ing at his establishment.

Gene Wallin, owner of
Rising Fawn Cafe

"They still park their trucks down there and walk around the fence," Wallin says. "That's because they know the food is good and everybody's friendly." Wallin, a former roofing contractor in Florida, returned to his hometown of Rising Fawn a few years ago and opened the restaurant with several of his relatives. The family owns peach and apple orchards and raises their own pigs and vegetables. The freshness and cooked-from-scratch quality was evident in the collard greens, coun-try-fried steak, and real mashed potatoes. Daily meat-and-three specials are $4.50.

Rutledge

The Yesterday Cafe

120 Fairplay Street (From Interstate 20, take Exit 49 and follow signs to Hard Labor
   Creek State Park.)
(706-557-9337)
Hours: Tuesday-Saturday, breakfast is served from 8:00 A.M.–11:00 A.M.; lunch is
   served Tuesday-Friday from 11:00 A.M.–2:00 P.M. and Sunday from 11:00 A.M.–
   3:00 P.M.; dinner is served Thursday from 5:00 P.M.–9:00 P.M. and Friday and
   Saturday from 5:00 P.M.–10:00 P.M.

If you drive through Rutledge by accident, you really are lost. This picturesque little town is in the middle of nowhere in the middle of Georgia. Antique shops abound, however, and you can get a fine Southern meal at The Yesterday Cafe. Located in a restored pharmacy, owners Alan and Teri Bragg's restaurant offers daily specials such as country-fried steak, mashed redskin potatoes with the skins, meat loaf, and an assortment of fresh vegetables. At night you need to dress up and bring more money as the meals get fancier and pricier. Prime rib, herbed catfish, fried shrimp, and fried oysters are among the dinner specials. For dessert, try the buttermilk pie made from a recipe that Teri found in her collection of old recipe books. Dieters can choose from a Caribbean salad made with marinated skinless chicken or a marinated grilled chicken sandwich. Prices range from under ten dollars for breakfast and lunch to ten to twenty dollars for dinner.

Savannah

"When I'm in Savannah, I like to eat at Lady and Sons. That's real Southern cooking. It's a buffet and it's very fattening, but I love it."

John Berendt, author of Midnight in the Garden of Good and Evil

Other Voices, Other Tastes

Mrs. Wilkes' Boarding House

By Kathy Hogan Trocheck

They still say the blessing over at Mrs. Wilkes' Boarding House in Savannah. It's a quiet prayer, usually, with heads bowed over all those steaming platters and bowls of fixings, but after you've tasted Sema Wilkes' fried chicken, barbecued pork, potato salad, green beans, biscuits, sweet-potato casserole, macaroni and cheese, and banana pudding, you may want to leap up and shout Hallelujah, or at least kneel in supplication to the saintly Southern matriarch who runs the place.

Photo by Jerry Bauer

I discovered Mrs. Wilkes as a bride, newly moved to that strangely insular Paris of the South—Savannah. A friend from the newspaper where we both worked took me there for lunch one day in 1976. At first, I didn't believe anybody still ran such a thing as a boardinghouse. The street, in the city's historic district, was mostly residential. There was no sign, no parking lot, just a white-uniformed waitress who sat outside snapping string beans.

An hour later, we trundled groggily up the steps and back down brick-paved Jones Street, swollen with chicken and biscuits and sweet tea and peach cobbler and I don't know what all. That's when I learned an important truth about lunch at Mrs. Wilkes'. Always plan for a nap afterwards. And wear pants with elastic. By dinnertime, say around midnight, you might feel up to some weak broth or saltine crackers.

Don't take your Mama, either. She'll get her feelings hurt when you rhapsodize about the tenderness of the biscuits, or the cool sweetness of the coleslaw, or the tangy bite of the barbecue sauce.

Since that first trip in 1976, I've taken dozens of visitors to Mrs. Wilkes'. Taking Yankees is the most fun. My friend, Jane, the New York vegetarian, holistic psychotherapist came to Savanah with me a few years ago. We traipsed around town doing the "Midnight in the Garden of Good and Evil Tour." I showed her the courthouse where the murder trial took place and the mansion on Monterey Square. We even visited Bonaventure Cemetery, where the famous bird-lady statue used to be located—until marauding tourists overran the place and the statue had to be put in storage.

It wasn't until we were sitting cheek-to-jowl with a tableful of strangers, handing around the chicken and dumplings and butter beans, sipping sweet tea, and exchanging friendly notes on Savannah that Jane got an inkling of what it is to be Southern.

We sat at that oilcloth-covered table, under the low ceilings and the careful watch of Mrs. Wilkes' family, and we became family, bonded by a love of good conversation, good talk and, of course, good manners. The last biscuit in the roll basket never did disappear. Nobody wanted to take the last one. And when we were done with that miraculous lunch, we stood up, cleared our own plates, and murmured thanks to the cashier.

"Now that's Southern," Jane said with a sigh.

Praise the Lord and pass the collards!

Mrs. Wilkes' Boarding House is located at 107 West Jones Street. (912-236-9816)

Kathy Hogan Trocheck is the Atlanta author of several mysteries, including *Midnight Clear* and *To Live and Die in Dixie*.

Social Circle

The Blue Willow Inn Restaurant
294 North Cherokee Road; Exit 47 off of Interstate 20 East
(770-464-2161)
Hours: Monday-Friday, 11:00 A.M.–2:30 P.M. and 5:30 P.M.–9:00 P.M.; Saturday,
11:00 A.M.–2:30 P.M. and 4:30 P.M.–9:00 P.M.; Sunday, 11:00 A.M.–9:00 P.M

This charming restaurant located in a 1907 Greek Revival mansion is about a forty-five-minute drive from Atlanta, but well worth the trip, both for the food and the history. The house was built by John Upshaw, an uncle of Margaret Mitchell's first husband, "Red" Upshaw. During their courtship when Upshaw was visiting his uncle, Mitchell stayed next door in a Victorian cottage.

If you visit the Blue Willow, I suggest you come hungry. The Southern buffet stretches around three walls of the large serving room and includes fried green tomatoes, fried chicken, baked ham, turkey and dressing, assorted other meats, and at least a dozen vegetables and salads. The stewed tomatoes are a trifle sweet for some tastes, but I found them delicious with the turnip greens, lima beans, squash, and mashed potatoes. Try the Southern pecan pie and peach cobbler for dessert, but add ice cream at your own peril. Afterward, you can take a stroll around the grounds to walk off some of the calories and visit the gift shop where they have souvenirs, cookbooks and, of course, Blue Willow china.

Thomasville

(Left to right) Sue Coleman, Mary Graham, and Betty Bryant of Market Diner

Market Diner
Next door to the Farmer's Market
(912-225-1777)
Hours: Monday-Thursday, 11:00 A.M.–9:00 P.M.; Friday and Saturday, 11:00 A.M.–10:00 P.M.; Sunday, 11:00 A.M.–4:30 P.M.

Thomasville is a lovely town just north of Tallahassee in prime quail-hunting country. Rich folks from Georgia and the North come here to dress up in their best L.L. Bean or Abercrombie & Fitch outfits and try to shoot birds out of the sky. Afterward, they return to white-columned plantation houses for Southern feasts of fried quail, fried chicken, and lightly sautéed vegetables. If you aren't the type to get invited to these hunts, don't worry. You can still eat like a Rockefeller for just a few dollars at the Market Diner in Thomasville. Next door to the Farmer's Market, John and Mary Graham's diner serves a buffet of four or five meat entrées, a dozen or more vegetables, and banana pudding and peach cobbler for around eight dollars. Night buffets are more expensive—about ten dollars—but on Friday and Saturday nights you can get all the seafood you can eat. And this is fresh-from-the-Gulf shrimp, mullet, oysters, and fish fried to a golden brown. On a typical day, I stopped in for lunch and pigged out on chicken livers, fried chicken, chicken and dumplings, country-fried steak, rutabagas, cabbage, macaroni and cheese, mashed potatoes, stewed corn, collards, and lima beans. (Well, I had to *sample* everything, didn't I?) The banana pudding was worth the price of the meal.

If you're in the mood for some *real* Southern food, come by on Thursday night. That's Old Timey Night and you'll find fried fatback, pork brains, pig feet, neck bones, chicken feet, chicken gizzards, and country ham and red-eye gravy on the buffet along with the pork-seasoned greens, cheese grits, and cracklin' cornbread. Yum!

The Market Diner also offers a full menu of items such as fried green tomatoes, fresh red roe (fish eggs), quail, amberjack, barbecue ribs, chicken livers, and hen and dressing.

Tucker

Matthews Cafeteria

2299 Main Street

(770-491-9577)

Hours: Monday-Friday, breakfast served from 4:30 A.M.–10:00 A.M.; lunch from
11:00 A.M.–3:00 P.M.; dinner from 4:30 P.M.–8:00 P.M.

Tucker is basically an Atlanta suburb, but it has the atmosphere of a small, rural town. This is especially true at Matthews Cafeteria, which is located in a nondescript concrete-block building across from Cofer Brothers Lumber Company. Here is where businessmen congregate for breakfast and lunch and families gather for dinner to eat the kind of food women in the South used to cook three times a day. Like any cafeteria, you pay by the item, usually $2.00 to $2.50 for meats and $1.00 for vegetables and desserts.

The day I had lunch at Matthews there was a choice of turkey and cornbread dressing, barbecued ribs, chicken livers, and beef tips. The mashed potatoes were real and the corn muffins were cooked the way God and Southerners intended them, without sugar. It was hard to pass up the deviled eggs, but the squash casserole, turnip greens, and creamed corn were too inviting. Fortunately, I saved room for the banana pudding prepared with real cooked-and-browned meringue. One small complaint: the chairs seem to be a trifle small and rickety, but maybe that's just my problem.

Watkinsville

Other Voices, Other Tastes
Gautreau's Cajun Cafe
Main Street Cafe

By Terry Kay

I am not, never have been, in fact, never will be a person who bounces around town trying out the new (or old) eateries. From my new home and surroundings in the Athens-Watkinsville area there are two places, both in Watkinsville, which feel right for me. One is Gautreau's Cajun Cafe, where one can actually find crawfish étouffée in the heart of barbecue country. I also suggest the sweet-potato chips with blue cheese; great stuff. The other feel-good spot for me in Watkinsville is the Main Street Cafe. Coffee, sandwiches, bagels, croissants, etc. A friendly, relaxed place.

Terry Kay is the author of *To Dance With the White Dog* and *The Runaway.*

Young Harris

Other Voices, Other Tastes
Mary Ann's

By Zell Miller

Mary Ann's is located on Main Street, Highway 76, next to the Young Harris Motel.

Mary Ann's is one of my favorite country cafes in Georgia, and it is right up the street from where I grew up in Young Harris. Breakfast is my favorite. A couple of eggs over easy with country ham or hand-patted-out sausage patties with grits and biscuits will knock your hat in the creek and make you forget all that fat-gram content stuff. Pancakes are good, too. For lunch, there is a buffet with all kinds of country-cooked vegetables and several meat choices. Save room for the apple cobbler or banana pudding.

And for dinner (called supper in Young Harris), try trout or pork chops. All the food is good and unbelievably inexpensive. You can look out the windows at the majesty of Double Knobbs Mountain, feel the slowed-down pace of Appalachia, check out some of the local characters and get the best and friendliest service you will ever experience.

And if this doesn't get me an extra biscuit at breakfast, I'll be disappointed.

Zell Miller is governor of Georgia and author of *Corps Values* and other books.

KENTUCKY

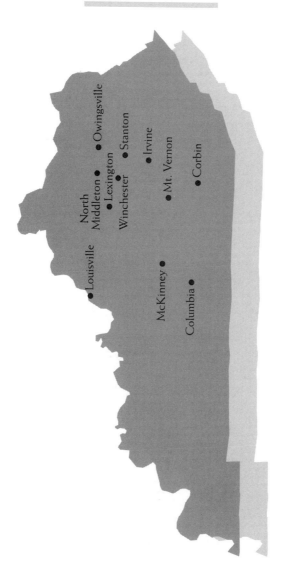

Owingsville •
Stanton •
Irvine •
North
Middleton •
Lexington •
Winchester •
Mt. Vernon •
Corbin •
Louisville •
McKinney •
Columbia •

This chapter on Kentucky restaurants was written by Susan Miller, a former restaurant critic for the *Lexington Herald-Leader* and the author of the *Insiders' Guide to Lexington*.

Columbia

Betty's OK Country Restaurant
2339 Campbellsville Road
(502-384-5664)
Hours: Monday-Saturday, 10:00 A.M.–1:00 P.M.; buffet from 10:30 A.M.–9:00 P.M.

You've got to put strong belief in any restaurant that spends three hours each day peeling potatoes like Betty's does. And that's when they only serve mashed potatoes. On days when home fries are served, too, it takes even more time and everybody in the kitchen takes a turn.

Betty's started out in a shoe-box of a building just on the outskirts of Columbia, but now owner Betty Ollestad has built another room and added attractive gray aluminum siding and some pretty landscaping. Country cooking reigns supreme here. People "go wild over the fried catfish and our homemade coleslaw," Betty says. And this is one of the only places you can find fried apples that are really fried instead of stewed. Betty's apples have plenty of color to them and a couple of people who weren't familiar with the wonderfully mushy and slightly caramelized fried version have even remarked that the apples were burned. Can you imagine!

The buffet has all the right stuff: casseroles, greens and beans, peas, beets, macaroni and tomatoes. In the dessert lineup, Betty's cream pies are known for their mile-high meringue, but it's the sand pie that's famous. "I tell people I go to Florida once a week and get the sand," she says. The sand pie is a layered concoction of crushed pecans and cookie crust, butter-pecan filling, whipped topping, cream cheese, and more pecans. Betty's also has a full menu and breakfast is served anytime.

Corbin

Dixie Restaurant
208 South Main Street
(606-523-1999)
Hours: Monday-Saturday, 6:00 A.M.–7:00 P.M.

You would think the novelty might wear off the "Dixie dog" after fifty years as a special at the Dixie Restaurant, but on any given day one hundred or more of them are served to local patrons who crowd in at lunchtime. The famous hot-dog sauce is cooked until almost all of the liquid is absorbed so it's sort of a flavored ground-beef sauce—which makes it pretty neat to eat. And one is never enough.

When you order a Dixie dog, it automatically comes with mustard and onions. You can also get a platter with slaw, French fries, or chips. Skipping the "dog" and just having a chili bun is another way to go.

This landmark downtown restaurant—which you can identify by the ruffled curtains at the front windows—would be a great home-style restaurant even without the Dixie dog. There's a lunch counter, a dozen or so vinyl-top tables, and the gray-painted paneling is a study in local sports photos: high-school football, basketball, and baseball teams. (Go Redhounds!) And the daily special is a belt-buster. It varies but it is usually something like meat loaf, mashed potatoes, green beans, cole-slaw, roll, and banana pudding. Breakfast (the works) is served all day, and a big variety of sandwiches is also available.

Irvine

Cedar Village Restaurant
206 Main Street
(606-723-7777)
Hours: Monday-Sunday, 10:00 A.M–10:00 P.M.

Since 1949 this restaurant has been dishing up "country cooking" to the locals, but since it moved into an attractive new building with modern booths, pretty wallpaper, modern light fixtures, and carpeting in the late 1980s, people drive from miles around for the big buffet in this little rural town. The best time to visit is Thursday through Sunday when there's a lot more to choose from. You can't go wrong anytime, but there's salmon croquettes and chicken and dumplings on Thursday, country ham and turkey and dressing on Saturday and Sunday. The cornmeal battered fish, meat loaf, stewed apples, and candied yams are out of this world, and the macaroni and tomatoes are an old-timey favorite along with a dozen or so other vegetables, including casseroles, brown or white beans, and green beans. And for dessert there might be rice pudding or bread pudding, double-chocolate cake, or a house specialty called a butter roll, which is a rich pie crust rolled up with cinnamon and nutmeg and served in a heated sauce. The buffet also includes a salad bar. You can also order off the menu, but your best bet is the buffet.

Lexington

Cummins & Sons Food Mart

6421 Athens-Boonesboro Road
(606-263-9427)
Hours: Monday-Saturday, 6:00 A.M.–6:00 P.M.

The sign out front that says "Billy's World Famous Chili Dogs" is a good tip-off. The chili dogs with homemade sauce are definitely worth the drive to this country store in the little community of Athens where the local farmers park their tractors and pickups out front and gather inside to talk about cattle and tobacco—or to just plain loaf. There are a couple of tables in back where there's always serious discourse about what's going on in the world but, more importantly, what's going on in the neighborhood. The hamburger-based sauce (without beans) is simple but addictive, and the hot dogs are popped in the microwave for a few sec-

onds so the finished product has a soft steamed bun. Onions and mustard make them just about perfect.

Billy's also serves a plate-lunch special every day. There's always spaghetti on Monday, but the rest of the week's menu depends on the whim of the cook. You might luck out and get there on banana-pudding day, but there's always homemade pie or cobbler. You can get breakfast and a full range of sandwiches with country ham, burgers, and tenderloin as the specialties with deviled eggs on the side. And in case you wonder what everybody is drinking out of those green bottles, it's the local drink called Ale-8-One, which is bottled in nearby Clark County. A lot of folks start their day out with an Ale-8 instead of a cup of coffee, so you can imagine the caffeine kick this soft drink has. If they don't recognize you at the store as a regular, they won't let you out the door until you try one.

Loudon Square Buffet
801 North Broadway
(606-252-9741)
Hours: Monday-Sunday, 10:00 A.M.–9:00 P.M.

This old place is a must-do. It's near a part of Lexington on the north side of town where no yuppie would dare tread. Going through the buffet line and piling an unbelievable variety of home-style fare mile-high on a green Melamine plate might not appeal to everyone, but if you're in the mood for a belt-busting meal, this is where to go.

The atmosphere in Loudon Square is definitely no frills. The old-fashioned room has booths with patched yellow vinyl, and plastic mustard containers add another dash of yellow to all the tables. But you're here for the food, not for decorating ideas.

On your first trip through the line (you have to go back at least once) try the sugar-and-vinegar coleslaw, brown beans, greens, stewed tomatoes so sweet they could pass for dessert, dressing and gravy, cornmeal-battered fish with tartar sauce, and corncakes. Still hungry? Did you forget the salads? There are three-bean salads, marinated vegetables, pickled beets, tossed salad, homemade potato salad, and Waldorf salad with miniature green marshmallows and apple chunks.

The vegetables are plentiful and generally good, although the mashed potatoes are instant. Meats include two kinds of chicken, ham in pineapple sauce, frankfurters, meatballs, and cornmeal-battered fish that's so good it's worth the trip.

Louisville

The interior of Andrew's

Andrew's

2286 Bardstown Road
(502-458-9421)
Hours: Monday-Friday, 8:00 A.M.–8:00 P.M.

If there was a prototype for diners, Andrew's would be it. It's the perfect little place, spic-and-span clean with creamy yellow walls, a lunch counter with stools that have wooden seats with slatted backs, an old-fashioned glass pie case, a few tables decked out with red oilcloth covers, and a steam table that holds treasures like butter beans, mustard greens, and black-eyed peas. You expect a waitress with a flowered hanky tucked in her uniform pocket and white service shoes to come sashaying out of the kitchen any second. And could that be Beaver and the Cleaver family over at the corner table?

There's breakfast every morning (scrambled eggs, sausage, and biscuits), but lunch and dinner are the highlights. Roast beef and chicken are served every day, but the rest of the menu goes like this: smoked sausage and kraut on Monday, fried chicken livers on Tuesday, country-fried steak on Wednesday, meat loaf on Thursday, salmon croquettes with dill sauce and chicken and noodles on Friday. And the variety of side dishes is amazing—fourteen in all, which is quite a production for a little place like this. For something really unique, try the butter-bean soup, and be sure to save room for cobbler.

McKinney

McKinney Depot
Busy Bee Street
(606-346-2222)
Hours: Monday–Thursday, 10:30 A.M.–8:00 P.M.; Friday, 8:00 A.M–8:30 p.m.; Sunday,
   11:30 a.m.–2:30 P.M.

The wooden building, which houses this busy backroad restaurant, was built as a replica of the old railroad station in the late 1800s, complete with a red caboose next door. There's not much activity in this little farming community these days, so the restaurant is a destination in itself—one that attracts people several counties away because it's a nice country drive and the food is topnotch.

The catfish grilled over an open flame is the big selling special on Friday night (though you can order it anytime), and the restaurant is known for its homemade sourdough bread. There's always a homey plate-lunch special which averages three dollars for lunch and about six dollars for dinner. But the belt-busting Sunday buffet is the highlight with fried chicken, corn pudding, green beans, and homemade rolls always. Other vegetables might include creamed peas, stewed apples, and macaroni and cheese. Biscuits and gravy are available all the time, and the restaurant makes its own hot-dog sauce and serves a big variety of sandwiches.

Mt. Vernon

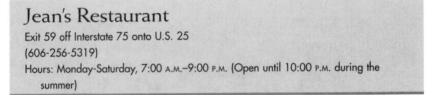

Jean's Restaurant
Exit 59 off Interstate 75 onto U.S. 25
(606-256-5319)
Hours: Monday–Saturday, 7:00 A.M.–9:00 P.M. (Open until 10:00 P.M. during the
   summer)

Perched on a hill at the top of a winding little road about a half-mile from the interstate, Jean's has been a landmark for the best pinto beans, made-from-scratch biscuits with milk gravy, and piping hot cornbread for more than forty years. It's a little roadside cafe with green-and-white wallpaper, vinyl-top tables, and captain's chairs—the kind of place where many of the locals go to eat every day. Roast turkey and cranberry sauce are served year-round, and the pork chops, fried potatoes, and fried apples should go down in the home-style hall of fame. And there's more. The mashed potatoes are real, and the chicken is pan-fried and served with milk gravy. Some folks go just for the fried chicken livers. The Renfro Valley complex, famous for the Renfro Valley Barn Dance, country-music shows, and an old-fashioned shopping village, is five minutes away. A  tip: the restaurant is tricky to find and is on an unmarked road. The best thing to do is stop at a gas station as soon as you exit the interstate and have them point it out for you. They're used to it.

North Middletown

The Skillman House

Main Street

(606-362-4348)

Hours: Tuesday-Thursday, 7:00 A.M.–6:00 P.M.; Friday and Saturday, 7:00 A.M.–
8:00 P.M.; Sunday, 7:00 A.M.–4:00 P.M.

This is surely the only restaurant around that is so homey you think you might need to knock on the front door before going in. If you took an old house, set up dining tables in the living room and dining room, and left all of the other furniture and knickknacks in, you'd have The Skillman House in this tiny community way off the beaten path. There's even a clawfoot tub in the bathroom. As for the food, it's the fried chicken and catfish that people eat "like it's going out of style" as well as lamb fries in cream gravy, says owner, cook, and server Katherine McGlothin. And the regulars come, sometimes a whole table of six, who order nothing but "Manhattans," a local specialty made with thin-sliced roast beef on white bread that is cut in half with a big mound of mashed potatoes in the middle, all smothered in brown gravy. (Just looking at it makes your cholesterol jump a dozen points.) There's a secret here, though. For a real good comfort-food fix, order a Manhattan made with cornbread instead of white bread. Whoo-ee!

And then there are the pies, which are displayed in an old glass-front bookcase: chocolate cream and buttermilk for $1.25. The regular menu includes sandwiches (even a fried-egg sandwich), as well as steaks, and breakfast is served daily. Entrées range from $4.00 to $9.00.

Owingsville

Green's Restaurant and Motel

U.S. 60 East via Interstate 64, east to the Owingsville-Salt Lick exit

(606-683-2151)

Hours: Monday-Saturday, 6:30 A.M.–8:00 P.M.

Until a few years ago, Green's was a vintage, time-worn diner connected to a six-room roadhouse motel that had been built in the 1940s. It once served as a Greyhound bus stop. But owner Barbara Powell, who has worked at the restaurant since she was thirteen, said when the restaurant started "going down the creek," she had to do a bit of remodeling. It's still a great country diner with an old lunch counter in front and tomatoes ripening in a window with a little ruffled curtain in the summertime. But the old wooden floors have been covered with vinyl and the outside has been spiffed up.

Green's serves the best roast beef and mashed potatoes, Swiss steak, pork tenderloin, and cornbread around. And if you're lucky, you might even get fried corn or chicken and dumplings and dressing. You can drive on down the road a few miles to Cave Run Lake to hike off the meal. A full menu is available and entrées range from five to six dollars.

Stanton

Bruen's Restaurant

South Sipple Street (When you come off the Mountain Parkway into Stanton, turn left next to the Dairy Queen.)

(606-663-4352)

Hours: Sunday-Thursday, 4:30 A.M.–8:30 P.M.; Friday and Saturday, 4:30 A.M.–
9:30 P.M.

No frills would be a bit of an understatement for this truly down-home restaurant located in a little, square concrete building with a window or two in the back. It's sort of a well-kept secret to outsiders because you have to peek in the front door to see if it's really a restaurant—and also to see if it's really open.

Actually, it's almost always open. The biscuits start coming out of the oven shortly after 4:30 A.M. every day and breakfast is served anytime. This is the kind of place where the locals gather to drink coffee and read the paper. And if you peek in the kitchen, you're sure to see grandmother types cooking up all this good food.

Bruen's has pecan-hued paneling, and the tables are decked out with flowered vinyl clothes. There's a doll collection in a big glass case, along with gumball machines and lots of knickknacks. And it just happens to serve the best pork tenderloin, deviled eggs, and cream pies for miles around. Natural Bridge State Park is nearby, so go for a big breakfast of country ham, eggs over easy, biscuits and gravy, and a glass of buttermilk, then take a long hike to wear it off. Maybe after that, you can go back for lunch (I'm only slightly kidding), or just for a cup of coffee and a slice of their famous pies—butterscotch, chocolate, and coconut—or blackberry cobbler.

Winchester

Cantuckee Diner

12 Carol Road
(606-744-7377)
Hours: Monday-Thursday, 8:00 A.M.–9:30 P.M.; Friday-Sunday, 8:00 A.M.–10:30 P.M.

If Daniel Boone could come back to Clark County for a visit, he undoubtedly would choose Cantuckee Diner for a Sunday dinner of chicken and dumplings. It might be a little hard to ride a horse down the bypass where the restaurant is located, but it would be worth it.

The specialties that keep the locals lined up at the door are fried catfish, barbecue (smoked on the premises), biscuits and gravy for breakfast, and daily specials such as chicken and dumplings and meat loaf. This is a no-frills place that you would never choose based on appearance. It's plain-looking outside and inside there are knotty-pine walls and wooden booths. This is also the kind of place where the sour cream and tartar sauce come in little plastic cups with lids, and the butter is wrapped squares. If you want an appetizer, one of the house specialties is fried banana peppers, tasty and milder than the Jalapeño poppers many restaurants serve. Cantuckee Diner offers burgers and sandwiches, but the lunches and dinners are the best choices. Regional favorites include country ham, chicken livers, country-fried steak, liver and onions, hot roast beef and mashed potatoes, and other daily specials. Side dishes include punchy coleslaw, stewed apples, and moist dressing seasoned with plenty of sage. A small catfish dinner features two big filets coated with a crunchy cornmeal batter that is just about as good as catfish gets. For dessert, the German chocolate cake is recommended. Unless they have blackberry cobbler on the menu, that is.

The Engine House Deli

9 West Lexington Avenue
(606-744-0560)
Hours: Monday-Saturday, 11:30 A.M.–
   9:00 P.M.

If it has to do with the past, you can find it at Bob Tabor's fire-station-turned-restaurant in downtown Winchester. Tables, chairs, old chrome stools at the lunch counter, restaurant equipment, even the jukebox came from old restaurants or honky tonks that used to be. To top that, some of the songs on the jukebox are from local musicians who made recordings back in the '60s.

To add to the nostalgia, there's a wood-burning stove back in one corner, cozy poplar paneling (the real thing) that Bob installed himself, and an old radio where folks can listen to Prairie Home Companion on Saturday night. When carry-out orders are called in, Bob answers on an old rotary-dial phone.

The interior of The Engine House Deli

As you might imagine, some of the recipes are old, too. The beer cheese alone is worth a trip, and it's no wonder because it's made from the recipe of Johnny Allman, who originated this spicy, garlicky Bluegrass specialty spiked with day-old beer decades ago at his legendary Allman's restaurant on the Kentucky River. (Bob says he uses fresh beer these days, though).

Another local specialty, the open-faced hot Brown sandwich (which originated at the Brown Hotel in Louisville), is traditionally made with toast, turkey, mornay sauce, with two bacon strips criss-crossed on top. But Bob gives it a sumptuous down-home twist by adding country ham, white cheddar cheese, and "country mornay" sauce, which is simply old-fashioned sausage gravy. It's a hot Brown gone native.

The chili is a winner, too, and it's made from an old recipe perfected by Ed Hall, another great cook from the past who was known by all the locals. And this restaurant surely serves the only boiled hamburger in the state. You heard it right—boiled, as in water. All the grease cooks out, so a lot of people just order two. To round things out, the spaghetti sauce is from an "old Italian grandmother," the real grandmother of a former partner in the restaurant.

There are also hoagies, pizzas, and plenty of sandwiches, including homemade pimento cheese and olive nut. And to go along with all these good things, order a beer or a bottle of Ale-8-One (bottled locally and referred to as Clark County Coffee because of its caffeine kick), which Bob stores in an old ice-cream freezer and serves with about an inch of ice on top so the locals practically fight over it. Just get the car keys!

Waterfront Cafe

220 Athens-Boonesboro Road
(606-527-3313)
Hours: Monday-Saturday, 8:00 A.M.–9:30 P.M. during the summer; the restaurant
closes around 7:30 P.M. in the winter.

Beer cheese and fried banana peppers originated in the area of Boonesboro on the Kentucky River so, naturally, folks still love to drive to "the river" for those two specialties. And it's even better when you find a place that has kept the rustic flavor of the neighborhood—a place with plenty of character like Waterfront Cafe.

The front section of Waterfront is a small grocery store with a few booths in the middle of the floor where you can get a quick bite.

But this is a place where you'll want to spend some time and rub elbows with the neighborhood regulars, so mosey on through the store to the bar in back, or outside to a big patio and deck which overlook the river. Put your order in for beer cheese and banana peppers right away if you're a newcomer. If you're a regular, you don't order. Owner Kathy Justice knows what you drink and eat, and she just brings it automatically.

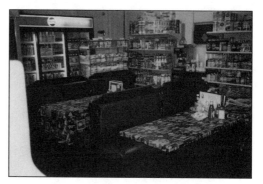

The interior of Waterfront Cafe

The next item on your agenda should be to throw a few quarters in the jukebox. Keep in mind this is a place where folks still dance to the jukebox—or to the music of the local band called the Moo Dogs that plays on weekends.

There's catfish on the menu but most of the regulars order the fried whitefish dinner with slaw, hush puppies, and a baked potato. There's always a homey special, too—maybe beans and potatoes and tenderloin, chicken pot pie, or pork-chop casserole. And the rib-eye steaks are a big seller, as well as fried chicken livers with cream gravy, frog legs, and lamb fries in season.

If you go on Thursday night, you must put your order in before 8 o'clock because about two hundred motorcycles come cruising into the parking lot "at exactly 8:32," says Kathy. Most of them stay for dinner, and the place is theirs for the rest of the night.

The cafe also serves a mean breakfast (eggs, biscuits, tenderloin, and hash browns), lunch every day, and burgers and sandwiches all the time. If you're in the area, Fort Boonesborough State Park is less than a five-minute drive.

LOUISIANA

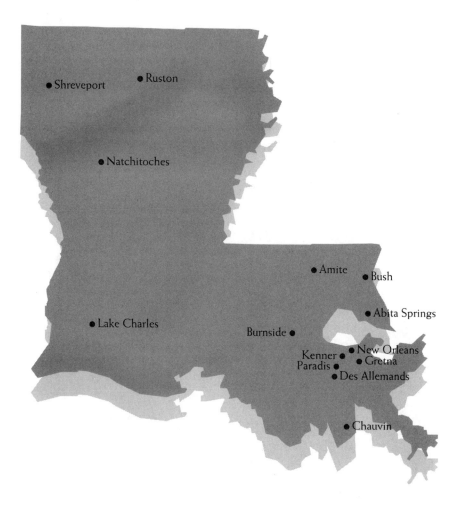

- Shreveport
- Ruston
- Natchitoches
- Amite
- Bush
- Abita Springs
- Lake Charles
- Burnside
- New Orleans
- Kenner
- Gretna
- Paradis
- Des Allemands
- Chauvin

Abita Springs

Abita Springs Cafe
22132 Level Street
(504-867-9950)
Hours: Tuesday-Friday, 8:00 A.M.–2:30 P.M.; Saturday and Sunday, 8:00 A.M.–
3:00 P.M.

Abita Springs was once a gathering place for Native Americans because of its natural springs. The Choctaw Indians used the water in medicinal treatments and created legends about its healing powers. Later, wealthy New Orleanians frequented the health resort. Now tourists come to enjoy the quiet beauty of the town, browse at the antique shops, sample the wares of the Abita Brewery and Brew Pub, and dine at the Abita Springs Cafe.

Lunch and dinner at the cafe are a notch above the usual country restaurants in the South. Maybe that's because owner Dean Boelens used to work at the famous Commander's Palace in New Orleans. Lunch specials include fried-catfish salad, shrimp, smoked sausage and tomatoes with tortellini pasta in a parmesan cream sauce, and grilled rib-eye on a bed of peas, onions, and potatoes in a creole meunière sauce. Although lunch is popular, Boelens admits that his breakfasts featuring Angel Biscuits draw the largest crowds. "We serve lots of omelettes—big omelettes—and waffles and pancakes, but people seem to like our biscuits the best," Boelens said. And no wonder. These light-as-air biscuits make cathead biscuits look like appetizers. They are the size of salad plates and so delicious they are almost a meal in themselves, especially if you get the biscuit and gravy. If you're really hungry, however, try the Abita Star breakfast special—a bed of hash browns topped with two eggs over easy, Swiss and American cheese, a sauce of diced ham, peppers, onions, and pimentos. Another popular breakfast, the pancake special, consists of an extra-large pancake topped with whipped cream and strawberries and pecans or bananas or blueberries. Come early, because the Abita Springs Cafe is basically a cottage with two small dining rooms, and space is limited.

Dean Boelens, owner of Abita Springs Cafe

Amite

Cabby's Restaurant
205 NW Central
(504-748-9731)
Hours: Monday-Saturday, 11:00 A.M.–10:00 P.M.; Sunday, 11:00 A.M.–2:00 P.M.

Amite is a pleasant enough little village, but it certainly seems to attract bad luck. Four catastrophes almost wiped out the town since it was founded in 1862. In 1903, a fire broke out one Sunday afternoon and destroyed the entire business section. Five years later, a cyclone struck, leveling many businesses, homes, and most of the churches. The next year a Gulf storm wreaked havoc for several days. And, in 1940, a tornado roared through town destroying nearly all of the businesses and causing much loss of life.

Apparently the residents were persistent and refused to leave. The main street today has a number of businesses, including a hodge-podge of buildings known as Cabby's Restaurant. Inside one section of the restaurant are the old brick walls and wooden floors of what formerly was a bank. A house next door has been attached and is used as a bar and dining area. Separate rooms are used for civic-club luncheons and other meetings.

Cabby's has an extensive menu with seafood, fried catfish, prime rib, and gumbo, but your best bet is to go there for the lunch buffet. At the buffet, you have a choice of red beans and rice, fried chicken, catfish, roast beef, chicken and dumplings, yams, greens, and other Southern vegetables. And if you're still hungry after all that, try Cabby's Mississippi Mud Pie, a sumptuous dessert made of chocolate cream cheese and whipped cream on a pecan-cookie crust.

Burnside

The Cabin
Highway 44 and Highway 22
(504-473-3007)
Hours: Monday, 11:00 A.M.–3:00 P.M.; Tuesday-Thursday, 11:00 A.M.–9:00 P.M.; Friday and Saturday, 11:00 A.M.–10:00 P.M.; Sunday, 11:00 A.M.–6:00 P.M.

The Cabin looks like a typical tourist attraction with a gift shop and antiques and souvenirs in the adjoining general store. Well, it is, and it isn't. There's real history to The Cabin, unlike some of the erected-overnight places at interstate exits. The building was one of the slave quarters on the Monroe Plantation. Now it's where you can get a variety of po' boys, including one called a pirogue. It's named for a kind of canoe that Louisianians used to navigate the bayous and swamps, and it's almost as big. The center of a huge loaf of bread is scooped out and filled with shrimp, fried fish pieces and oysters, and any accompaniments you prefer. As a side dish, you have a choice of French fries, coleslaw, or red beans and rice.

Other po' boys offer fillings of sausage, roast beef, ham, and barbecued beef. And while you're there, check out the jambalya, gumbo, shrimp creole, or bread pudding. Other specials include down-home lunches of pork chops and fried chicken with assorted vegetables.

Bush

House of Seafood Buffet
Highway 21
(504-886-2231)
Hours: Thursday-Saturday, 4:00 P.M.–10:00 P.M.

The House of Seafood Buffet is just what it says. For about sixteen dollars, you can eat your fill of oysters on the half-shell, boiled crabs, crawfish, shrimp, king-crab claws, boudin, alligator sausage, stuffed or fried oysters, soft-shell crabs, fried fish, scallops, frog legs, and shrimp. Whew! And that's only the beginning. In the midst of all this seafood you have fried sweet corn, fried okra, fried yams, stuffed Jalapeño peppers, and broccoli au gratin. And of course, a Louisiana meal wouldn't be complete without étouffée, jambalaya, or gumbo.

All of the fried foods are delicious, but here's a little tip I learned from my cousin Bubba, who is a great connoisseur of all-you-can-eat places. If you stick to the boiled or steamed seafood, you don't fill up as quickly, and you get your money's worth.

Chauvin

La Trouvaille
4696 Highway 56
(504-873-8005)
Hours: Wednesday and Friday, 11:30 A.M.–2:00 P.M., October through May. (Other times available for tour groups who call ahead a day or two in advance)

La Trouvaille is one of the most interesting eating places you'll find in Louisiana. Located in an old house with one small sign out front, the restaurant is easily missed. As mentioned above, serving hours are limited to two days a week unless you're part of a large group. Then the Dusenberys will come out and whip up a special Cajun meal just for you.

Inside, the brightly painted walls and colorful tablecloths in the separate dining rooms create a cheerful atmosphere whether you are dining alone or with a party of twelve.

An old-time Cajun Sunday dinner is served the first Sunday of the month at 11:30 A.M. with afternoon entertainment by the Dusenbery family and friends. Reservations are required. On these Sundays, you'll have chicken gumbo, cooked rump roast, four-meat rice dressing, Cajun sweet peas, potato salad, candied yams, vanilla ice cream, coffee, and homemade root beer. Other times the menu includes shrimp étouffée or jambalaya, green beans with potatoes, eggplant fritters, tossed salad, dessert (bread pudding with meringue or tarte à la bouille—old-time custard pie). La Trouvaille means "a lucky find" in French, and once you've eaten there, you'll agree.

Des Allemands

Spahr's
Highway 90
(504-758-1602)
Hours: Monday-Thursday, 10:00 A.M.–9:30 P.M.; Friday-Sunday, 10:00 A.M.–
  10:00 P.M.

Whenever you see a restaurant's parking lot overflowing, chances are it's a pretty good place to eat. Maybe that's why I had to circle the lot twice at Spahr's to find a parking spot. Inside, the restaurant is large and comfortable, just right for casual dining. Owners Bill and Thelma Spahr do wonders with fried seafood and plate-lunch specials, but I recommend the catfish sauce piquant or the alligator sauce piquant. These are dishes with pieces of catfish or alligator seasoned with a spicy Cajun red sauce. Just make sure you have a large beverage before you try it. All of the seafood is good here, mainly because it's fresh and not overcooked. Also recommended: the gumbo and the bread pudding.

Gretna

Rick's Cafe
89 Westbank Expressway
(504-361-4354)
Hours: Monday-Saturday, 6:30 A.M.–
  10:30 P.M.; Sunday, 10:30 A.M.–
  9:00 P.M.

Several people recommended Rick's Cafe, and I'm grateful that they did. Just across the river from New Orleans, Rick's has been in business for more than forty years and is usually jammed with locals for breakfast and lunch. Breakfast is the most popular meal of the day, with everything you expect in the South (biscuits, ham, grits, eggs, pancakes, etc.), but I found lunch to be one of the best I had on this trip. The smothered pork chops on rice were so tender you could cut them with a fork. As a side order, I had a cup of the other special—large, dried lima beans with ham and smoked sausage. I was tempted to hang around for several more days to try the other daily specials such as the black-eyed peas and sausage, red beans and rice, grilled calf liver smothered in onions, the shrimp stew, or the select Louisiana oysters fried in corn flour. Specials come with a vegetable of the day. This is true comfort food, and I highly recommend it to anyone in search of great home cooking.

If you happen by in the evenings, however, things get a little fancier with seafood dinners, steaks, and Italian specialties such as shrimp-and-eggplant casserole and baked lasagna. You can get a seafood platter with butterfly shrimp, fried oysters, catfish filets, hush puppies, and a crab cake for about twelve dollars.

Kenner

Short Stop Po' Boys
4041 Williams Boulevard
(504-443-3211)
Hours: Monday-Thursday, 9:00 A.M.–8:00 P.M.; Friday and Saturday 9:00 A.M.–
9:00 P.M.

Sometimes you don't have to wander too far off the beaten path to get a good meal. Short Stop Po' Boys is in a strip shopping mall not far from the New Orleans airport. And while it doesn't have the tradition and ambiance of "Mother's" in New Orleans, it does have some mighty tasty sandwiches for reasonable prices. You can get a small, regular, or king po' boy with catfish, oysters, shrimp, or crayfish tails. The ingredients are fresh and fried crispy with hot sauce and pickles. Other recommendations: the hot-sausage patty or hot-sausage-link po' boy. I cannot get enough oyster po' boys, but I have to admit that the roast-beef sandwich here is probably one of the best I've eaten. The beef is delicately seasoned and cooked with homemade natural gravy, the kind you love to dip your bread in. As side orders, chicken and sausage gumbo is available every day, but you can only get seafood gumbo on Fridays.

Lake Charles

Other Voices, Other Tastes

Cajun Charlie's

James Lee Burke

Cajun Charlie's on Interstate 10 in Lake Charles, Louisiana, has an all-you-can-eat cajun buffet for $6.95. They've got catfish, greens with sausage and onions, and they've got this wonderful jambalaya made with chicken fat and sausage. It'll clog up your arteries. Shoot, it could clog up a sewer, but it's great. Cajun Charlie's is nothing fancy, just a typical blue-collar place. I eat there every chance I get.

James Lee Burke is the author of *Cadillac Jukebox* and eight other Dave Robicheaux mysteries set in Louisiana.

Natchitoches

Lasyone's Meat Pie Kitchen
622 Second Street
(318-352-3353)
Hours: Monday-Saturday, 7:00 A.M.–9:00 P.M.

Natchitoches is the oldest settlement in Louisiana, and the meat pies that Lasyone's sells have a tradition that goes back to the eighteenth century. A meat pie is a well-seasoned mixture of beef and pork with onions that is wrapped up in a half-moon pastry and fried—just like the fried fruit pies your Mama used to make. Meat pies are the specialty here, but don't overlook the rest of the menu—luscious, crisp fried catfish and other seafood, red beans and rice and sausage, chicken and dumplings, and banana pudding. The banana pudding is wonderful, but if you want an unusual treat, try the Cane River cream pie. Instead of yellow cake or white cake, the Lasyones use gingerbread for a spicier taste. If the town looks familiar, maybe it's because the movie *Steel Magnolias* was filmed here.

New Orleans

Causey's Country Kitchen
7245 Chef Menteur Highway
(504-242-2604)
Hours: Monday-Saturday, 6:00 A.M.–9:00 P.M.

Causey's is a few miles from the heart of the city, but it's well worth the trip. The restaurant didn't look like much from the outside, but the crowded parking lot told me I was at the right place, even if I was the only white customer. Inside, you take a seat at the counter or find one of the few vacant tables. If you've never had soul food, this is where you can sample the entire spectrum, from chitterlings (sometimes known as chitlins, but they're still hog intestines) to pork neck bones, and pig feet with rice. For those with less

Lattie Causey, Jr., serves a customer

exotic tastes, owner Lattie Causey, Sr., and son Lattie Causey, Jr., serve daily specials of red beans and rice with smoked sausage, smothered pork chops with mustard greens, fried chicken, meat loaf, barbecue ribs, black-eyed peas, smothered okra and rice, potato salad, collard greens, fried okra, baked macaroni, and cabbage.

I confess I didn't try the chitterlings, but the pork neck bones and the red beans and rice were some of the best I ever had. And, yes, I've had pork neck bones before. The finest part of the meal, however, was a slice of sweet-potato pie that was heavenly. Next trip I'll try the pig feet and chitterlings. I promise.

Dooky Chase's Restaurant

2301 Orleans Avenue
(504-822-9506)
Hours: Sunday–Thursday, 11:30 A.M.–11:00 P.M.; Friday and Saturday, 11:30 A.M.–
   midnight

The first time I asked directions to Dooky Chase's, the hotel clerk stared at me blankly. "It's on OR-le-ans," I repeated. Finally she laughed. "Oh, you mean Or-LEANS. Yeah, I know where that is." It's all a matter of learning to speak the language, and in New Orleans they have a language of their own. If you don't know the meaning of étouffée, gumbo, jambalaya, or beignet, you're at a cultural and culinary disadvantage. Étouffée (pronounced et-too-fay), by the way, means "smothered" in

French. In other words, the vegetables and seasonings are cooked in a rich seafood stock and then shrimp or crawfish are added. Gumbo is a thick soup made with a savory broth that is simmered for hours with okra, tomatoes, and a roux, which is a kind of gravy made with flour and pork fat, and thickened with filé powder from ground sassafras roots. Other ingredients such as crawfish or shrimp are added according to the chef's taste. Jambalaya is rice cooked with chicken and andouille (pronounced an-DO-we) sausage, vegetables, and seasonings. A beignet is a fried doughnut without a hole that is dipped in powdered sugar and is wonderful with chickory-laced coffee.

So much for the Creole culinary primer. At Dooky Chase's you can get creole gumbo or okra gumbo. The spicy sausage and seafood gumbo is so good you'll want to inhale it. I also recommend any of his fried-chicken plates, his chicken livers, or his seafood. For less than five dollars, you can get a three-piece chicken plate (lower parts) and French fries or vegetable of the day with a tomato salad. Sandwiches include hot sausage, pork chop, veal cutlet, shrimp, stuffed crab, catfish filet, or oysters.

Mother's Restaurant

401 Poydras Street
(504-523-9656)
Hours: Monday-Saturday, 5:00 A.M.–10:00 P.M.; Sunday, 7:00 A.M–10:00 P.M.

For more than half a century, Mother's has been known for serving good food at reasonable prices. Established in 1938 by Simon A. Landry, the restaurant became popular with the military and later attracted hordes of office workers and businessmen for breakfast and lunch.

Service is cafeteria style, and the lines form early. For breakfast, Mother's serves the usual eggs, biscuits, or pancakes along with grits and debris. No, not that kind of debris. This debris is the pieces of roast beef that fall in the gravy while baking in the oven. You can also get black ham, the crisp caramelized crust from Mother's baked ham, or fried ham.

Lunch is a mad scramble among the local business folks to get inside before the line gets too long. Specialties are po' boys, huge sandwiches filled with ham, roast beef, turkey, pork chops, chicken, Italian sausage, shrimp, fish, oysters, soft-shell crabs, or calamari. Or you can get the Famous Ferdi Special, which is a combination of baked ham, roast beef, debris and gravy, shredded cabbage, pickles, mayo, yellow and creole mustards. These sandwiches are delicious but messy. Don't wear your best Armani suit when you eat here.

In addition to sandwiches, Mother's offers turtle soup with sherry, gumbo, crawfish and shrimp étouffée, jambalaya, and an assortment of seafood platters. And by all means don't leave without trying the bread pudding, sweet-potato pie, or the peach pie.

Robin's on Canal
2501 Canal Street
(504-821-9800)
Hours: Monday-Sunday, 5:30 A.M.–2:00 P.M.

If you survive a night on Bourbon Street, the next morning you may want to drive a few blocks up Canal Street and get a wake-up meal at Robin's. (The owner's name is Robin Williams, but she is no relation to the comedian). That is, if you can face a plateful of eggs sunnyside-up or one of Robin's famous omelettes. (The house omelette is a combination of ham, bacon, sausage, green peppers, onions, mushrooms, and cheddar cheese, but you can also get a seafood omelette or chili-cheese omelette.) Also on the menu are eggs cooked your way with everything from bacon to calves liver. Daily lunch specials for the late risers are also delicious. Entrées include red beans and rice, pork chops, spaghetti and meatballs, or seafood, with cabbage, white beans, mustard greens, or other vegetables of the day.

Paradis

Tatum's Restaurant

15264 Highway 90 East
(504-758-1600)
Hours: 5:00 A.M.–midnight, seven days a week.

Tatum's is by no means picturesque—just a plain, functional cafe that emphasizes food over interior decorating. If you're a crawfish connoisseur, stop by on Friday, Saturday, or Sunday evenings and get 2½ pounds of the boiled critters for seven dollars. Afterward, wander over to the bar and listen to the country-music band du jour.

Lunches change daily. You can get a choice of catfish, white beans, mustard greens, steak and gravy, roast beef, pot roast, mashed potatoes, green beans, chicken and sausage gumbo, crawfish stew, hamburger steak with white or brown gravy, salad, tea, and dessert.

Ruston

Sarah's Kitchen

607 Lee Avenue
(318-255-1226)
Hours: Daily from 11:00 A.M.–7:00 P.M.

By John T. Edge

Every day, thousands of motorists whiz by Sarah's Kitchen, unaware of the quirky culinary treasures that await just a few blocks off Interstate 20 in a lower-middle-class neighborhood of tidy, clapboard houses on the fringes of Ruston. Don't make the same mistake. From the street, a large, hand-painted sign, set amidst a riot of flowers, cast-off iron stoves, and old radiators, proclaims Sarah's philosophy in no uncertain terms:

"Welcome to the world of no cans or boxes." Take this as an invitation to eat.

Sarah Albritton is indeed a stickler for fresh foods. On any given day four to five meats and thirteen to fifteen fresh vegetables are offered. Among the latter, turnip greens, black-eyed peas, okra and tomatoes, and sweet potatoes are menu mainstays. If you're lucky, Sarah will be serving her special sweet-and-sour squash, a hybrid she developed in her own back yard.

The restaurant interior is a study in sensory overload. Every surface of the ramshackle, wooden building is covered with mementos of Sarah's culinary career. Proclamations from the Louisiana governor's office share wall space with tributes printed by the Smithsonian Institution. African tribal art is stacked in a dark corner.

Yet, all is overshadowed by Sarah's visionary paintings, which sit on easels awaiting a break in the business day. Between batches of "hot-water" cornbread, she puts down her spatula and picks up a brush, working feverishly on color-saturated interpretations of simpler times past and apocalyptic times to come.

—*Oxford, Mississippi, resident John T. Edge, who writes authoritatively about food for the* Oxford American *and* Southern Living, *is at work on a book of Southern foodways titled* The Southern Culture Cookbook. *Sarah's Kitchen and Herby K's are two of his favorite restaurants in Louisiana.*

Shreveport

Herby K's

1833 Pierre Avenue
(318-424-2724)
Hours: Monday-Thursday, 11:00 A.M–9:00 P.M.; Friday and Saturday, 11:00 A.M.–
10:00 P.M.

By John T. Edge

In a derelict neighborhood where most of the other businesses either burned up or boarded up long ago, this Shreveport institution endures. Famous since 1936 as the home of the "Shrimp Buster"—a faux sandwich of four butterfly shrimp, perched atop buttered French bread and served with a side of special sauce—Herby K's is as appreciated for the eccentricities of its ribald staff as for its frosty cold fishbowls of beer and delicately fried soft-shell crabs.

Though there is a tree-shaded beer garden on the side of the building, I prefer to sit inside at one of the four booths or six stools. Inside, you're a part of the action, free to trade jokes with the owner, reminiscences of meals past with a fellow patron, or insults with a waiter. (On my last trip, my waiter, Killer, warned the four shrimp on my plate that I would be eating them. When I asked why, he said, "They were alive yesterday; don't you think they deserve the courtesy?")

The menu is short. The prices are ridiculously low. And the atmosphere is a heady mix of flea-market castoffs and family heirlooms. Don't expect pretense and you won't be disappointed. In search of a wonderful meal far from the maddening milieu of chain restaurants? Relax. You've found the best seafood in Shreveport.

—Oxford, Mississippi, resident John T. Edge, who writes authoritatively about food for the Oxford American *and* Southern Living, *is at work on a book of Southern foodways titled* The Southern Culture Cookbook. *Sarah's Kitchen and Herby K's are two of his favorite restaurants in Louisiana.*

MISSISSIPPI

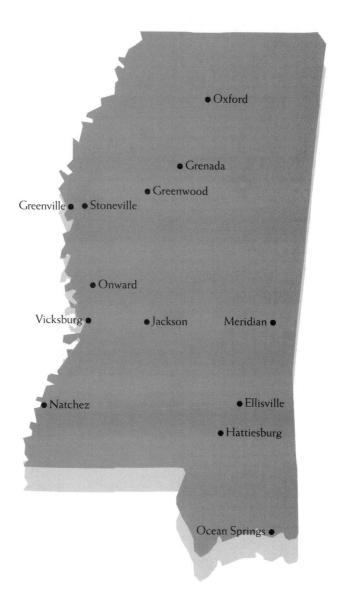

- Oxford

- Grenada

- Greenwood

Greenville - - Stoneville

- Onward

Vicksburg - - Jackson   Meridian -

- Natchez   - Ellisville

- Hattiesburg

Ocean Springs -

Ellisville

Fanny and Herchel Price, owners of Country Girl Kitchen

Country Girl Kitchen

807 Hill Street
(601-477-8191)
Hours: Monday-Thursday, 4:00 A.M.–5:00 P.M.; Friday, 4:00 A.M.–11:00 P.M.;
   Saturday, 4:00 A.M.–1:00 P.M.

From the outside, the Country Girl Kitchen looks like a building that's about to be condemned. The inside is a little better, but certainly nothing Martha Stewart would ever set foot in. An assortment of wobbly dinette tables and chairs are bunched together in a dimly lit room with lots of pictures and signs with wise sayings. My favorite is the one that reads: "FOR SALE. Complete Set of Encyclopedias. My Wife Knows Everything." Once your eyes adjust to the dimness, meander over to your right and take a look at the buffet. For four dollars, you can fill your plate with chicken and dumplings, fried chicken, hominy, cabbage, baby lima beans, greens, cornbread, and the dessert of the day. I took a moderate helping of each since I had a big breakfast, but owner Fanny Price jerked the plate out of my hand at the cash register with the comment "You ain't got enough there to keep a bird alive," and went back and ladled on more food. I ate it all just to be polite.

As I was eating, I noticed two older gentlemen that looked like they were dressed for roles in *Deliverance* sitting nearby. One eyed me suspiciously and asked what my business was. I told him and he brightened.

"These are the best butter beans I've had in years," I said, groping for common conversational ground. "I grew 'em myself," he responded. "I grow all the vegetables for this place." He smiled. "Have to. I'm married to the woman that owns it." He introduced himself as Herchel Price, stated proudly that he had been married to Fanny for fifty-three years, and began bragging about his grandchildren. Once again, it just goes to show you that appearances are deceiving, and you really can't judge a restaurant by its decor.

Greenville

Doe's Eat Place

502 Nelson Street
(601-334-3315)
Hours: Monday-Saturday, 5:00 P.M.–
    9:00 P.M. (or later, depending on the
    crowd); takeout (tamales only) from
    9:00 A.M.–9:00 P.M.

Charles Signa (left) and Doe Signa, Jr., owners of Doe's Eat Place

Doe's isn't much to look at on the outside. It resembles nothing more than a rundown beer joint in a rundown part of town. Doe's isn't much to look at on the inside either, a hodge-podge of rooms and huge stoves turning out enormous steaks and tamales for clientele that ranges from the poorest Greenvillians to senators and congressmen. Steaks are a cholesterol-watcher's nightmare. The smallest is twenty-eight dollars for a two-pound steak and fifty dollars for about a six-pounder. Owners Charles Signa and Doe Signa, Jr., assured me these are intended for sharing. Unless you're like my friend Paul Howle, who insists he has eaten a five-pound roast in one sitting.

Other Voices, Other Tastes

By Willie Morris

I have many favorite restaurants in the great and sovereign state of Mississippi, but I'll single out Doe's Eat Place in Greenville because it's the establishment JoAnne and I drive the farthest to from Jackson just to have dinner. The atmosphere is, to put it mildly, rustic. The famous journalist David Halberstam was in Greenville some years back on a lengthy assignment and when some local people brought him in through the kitchen door of Doe's, his temptation was to leave on the spot. Instead, after having dined there, he came back sixteen nights in a row.

I prefer a table in the kitchen where I absorb the vivid banter of the cooks and waitresses. The tamales are superlative, the French fries ineffable, and the T-bone steaks phantasmagoric. The atmosphere is so congenial that people at other tables finish your sentences for you.

A native of Yazoo City, Mississippi, Willie Morris is the author of a number of books, including *North Toward Home*, *My Dog Skip*, and *The Ghosts of Medgar Evers*.

Gus's Family Restaurant

1660 Highway 1 South
(601-335-4712)
Hours: Tuesday-Thursday, 10:30 A.M.–9:00 P.M.; Friday, 10:30 A.M.–10:00 P.M.;
    Saturday, 6:00 A.M.–10:00 P.M.; Sunday, 6:00 A.M.–9:00 P.M.

Gus's has been an institution in Greenville for thirty-five years, and for good reason. Owners Sidney Warren, Kathe Warren, and Pat Jennings serve fresh vegetables and meats for a reasonable price. Lunch specials of a meat and three vegetables, a drink, and dessert are seven dollars. And in addition to the usual country-fried steak and fried chicken, you can get shrimp fettucini or roast beef. Or you can load up on vegetables such as speckled butter beans, mustard greens, macaroni and cheese, squash casserole, and broccoli casserole. But if you're going there on a Sunday, I recommend the chicken and dressing. It's wonderful and goes real well with the broccoli casserole, despite what disparaging remarks George Bush made about this tasty green vegetable. Maybe if George had eaten at Gus's he would have changed his mind.

Jim's Cafe

314 Washington Avenue
(601-332-5951)
Hours: Monday-Saturday, 5:00 A.M.–
    7:00 P.M.

Jim's is one of those downtown cafes that used to be on every town square in the South. Owner Gus Johnson's family has been operating the restaurant for fifty years in the same location despite the changing economic conditions of Greenville. With the coming of the casinos a few blocks away, business has picked up, Gus said. "The casinos don't start going good until around six or so, and we've been open all day. We get a lot of the casino workers who are tired of the buffets over there and come here for some good vegetables."

*Ola Mae Cross and Gus Johnson
from Jim's Cafe*

Jim's serves varying lunch specials such as country-fried steak and gravy with rice and two vegetables. Vegetables include turnip greens (picked fresh and not frozen), corn, field peas and snaps, potatoes au gratin, and pineapple ring with cheese. Dessert comes with the meal, and if you're smart you'll get the banana pudding.

The walls of Jim's are covered with historic photographs of the town and of Gus Johnson's friends. The booths are comfortable, and nobody comes to chase you away if you want to dawdle over coffee at breakfast. In fact, my waitress Ola Mae Cross was so friendly I was tempted to stay until dinner and eat some of Jim's famous fried oysters. (I was swayed to leave, however, when Gus informed me he was out of oysters and waiting for a fresh shipment.)

One downside to breakfast is that Jim's, like other mom-and-pop places, have resorted to using little packets of powdered coffee creamer instead of the real stuff. But that was offset by the jelly. Miss Ola Mae brought me a big jar of homemade muscadine jelly and set it on the table with a spoon. This probably violated any number of health codes, but after a couple of spoonfuls on my biscuit I felt as if I were back home.

Greenwood

Lusco's
722 Carrolton Avenue
(601-453-5365)
Hours: Tuesday-Saturday, 5:00 P.M.–10:00 P.M.

Lusco's may be a little pricey to be included in this kind of guide, but the unique, shabby gentility of Andy and Karen Pinkston's restaurant—as well as the quality of the food—makes this a must-visit place. Don't be deceived by the outward appearance of Lusco's. It began as a grocery store in 1933 in downtown Greenwood, and it still looks like the kind of rundown, faded-brick establishment you still see in decaying towns all over the South. The location is not in the best part of town, either. The original Lusco's evolved from grocery store to restaurant when Charles and Marie Lusco and their three daughters added

Karen Pinkston, who owns Lusco's with her husband Andy

partitioned booths at the rear for dining. (These banquettes also provided a private place for cotton planters to drink Papa Lusco's home brew with their friends). These curtained, individual dining rooms with peeling, medicine-green walls and cloud-white tablecloths are still one of the charming attractions of Lusco's. Each is large enough for a table of six or so and is very private. Business boomed during World War II, when troop trains stopped on the tracks directly across from the restaurant and soldiers came in for platters of seafood. The meals were so memorable that the soldiers spread the word wherever they were stationed. Later, during good years for cotton farmers, wealthy planters and businessmen brought guests to Lusco's for special occasions. Now owned by a third generation of Lusco descendants, the restaurant attracts most of its customers from outside the Greenwood area and from as far away as Jackson and Memphis. Some drive a hundred miles or so because of tradition; the rest do it for the food—the freshest seafood north of the Gulf. The Pinkstons and their staff delicately fry or broil red snapper, catfish, and shrimp. The sirloin steak is described as being "as tender as a mother's love," and it is. Regulars swear by the pompano, available only in season, and broiled in lemon-butter sauce. I had the

One of the curtained private dining rooms at Lusco's. To the left is a framed story that Willie Morris wrote on a tablecloth.

broiled catfish with crab meat, a cup of gumbo that was spicy hot and wonderful, and an appetizer of broiled shrimp, garlic toast, and kumback sauce. Just dip your shrimp and your toast in the sauce and pretend you've died and gone to heaven. The fried onion rings and French fries are hand-cut and deliciously non-greasy. Even the salads are marvelous here, especially Lusco's Mediterranean salad with mixed greens, capers, ripe olives, purple onions, and feta cheese. If you still have room for dessert, the Oreo cheesecake or the chocolate sin are waiting for you. As I said, Lusco's ain't cheap (twenty to thirty dollars for entrées and appetizer), but compared to a comparable restaurant in a big city, it's a bargain.

Grenada

Sister's Catfish and Steak House
Highway 8 East, four miles from Interstate 55
(601-226-6556)
Hours: Thursday, 4:00 P.M–9:00 P.M.; Friday, 4:00 P.M.–10:00 P.M.; Saturday,
    4:00 P.M.–10:00 P.M.; Sunday, 11:00 A.M.–4:00 P.M.

Irene Henson is the sister in Sister's Catfish and Steak House. For more than eight years she has been feeding the folks of Grenada all-you-can-eat buffets of catfish, and for eight years they keep coming back for more. There's no reason to get anything other than the catfish (served whole or in fillets, they are fried golden brown and never taste greasy), but you can order other things from the menu.

Sister's offers sirloin, T-bone, and rib-eye steaks, hamburgers, oysters, barbecue, beef tips, shrimp, and boiled or fried chitterlings. Yes, that's right. Boiled or fried chitterlings with French fries and slaw. I politely asked Irene if chitterlings were a big seller in Grenada. Being a no-non-

The staff at Sister's

sense woman she snorted and said, "If they didn't sell, I wouldn't keep them on the menu." Sunday lunch is a little different. That's when the church crowd comes in for chicken and dumplings, chicken and dressing, and hamburger steaks.

Miss Clara's

131 Main Street
(601-226-4422)
Hours: Monday-Friday, 7:00 A.M.–2:00 P.M.

By Carolyn O'Brien

Last October a sign in the window of Miss Clara's read "Miss Mississippi Eats Here." Of course, that's mainly due to the fact that the owners of Miss Clara's are Myra Barginear's parents. Myra was the reigning Miss Mississippi for 1998. Richard and Rhonda Barginear's celebrity daughter is not what has brought in the crowds since its opening in 1985, however. It is the consistently good food, excellent service, and warm ambiance. Miss Clara's Cafe was founded by Lynn and Marilyn Rose and named after Lynn's grandmother. The Barginears acquired Miss Clara's in 1994. The name stayed the same, and so did many of the recipes. The homemade vegetable soup and cornbread is made from a recipe handed down from Miss Clara herself, along with the recipes for homemade pies such as buttermilk, brownie fudge, crusty coconut, caramel chess, and pecan.

Miss Clara's offers a traditional country breakfast including homemade biscuits and grits. The plate-lunch specials are posted daily on a blackboard inside the restaurant, or you can order from the menu. The most expensive item on the menu, by the way, is the low-fat meal—baked chicken breast, baked potato, and tossed salad with tea or coffee for $4.75.

I recommend the pies, but if you're too full for dessert, you can sip a cup of coffee or cappuccino and enjoy the wide assortment of customers—executives, teachers, hunters, lawyers, construction workers, and someone's great aunt who actually attended finishing school in Natchez.

In 1997, by popular vote, the citizens of Grenada gave Miss Clara's the designation "Best Lunch in Town" and "Best Sweet Tea in Town." Now that's a combination that's impossible to beat.

—*Carolyn O'Brien owns Books, an independent bookstore in Grenada, Mississippi.*

Hattiesburg

Nanny's Country Kitchen

907 Edwards Street
(601-583-1117)
Hours: Monday-Friday, 10:30 P.M.–2:30 P.M.

The Nanny in Nanny's Country Kitchen is Barbara Walter, who, with her daughter Mary Meadows, opened the restaurant in 1988. The women were forced to find another way of making a living after they had to close the family furniture business when Mary's husband became ill. "We prayed about it, and the Lord told us to open a restaurant," Mary said. The only culinary experience they had was cooking for their own families, so naturally the first few weeks were a real shock. "We didn't know how much to cook," Mary said, "so we kept running out of food." The other thing they learned, besides estimating the quantities, was to make the dishes consistent. "Folks don't want you experimenting every week so that the squash casserole tastes different," Mary said.

Nanny Walter (left) and Mary Meadows with a pan of freshly baked yeast rolls

After ten years, the women seem to have gotten it right. Although the restaurant is in a remote and run-down part of town, dozens of blue-collar workers and businessmen come in every day to see what's on the cafeteria line. There's always some kind of chicken, fried or baked, and an assortment of other entrées such as fried pork chops, chicken creole, or hamburger steak. The cornbread dressing is moist and properly seasoned with just a touch of sage, and the mashed yams were not excessively sweet. Also recommended is the spinach casserole and the banana pudding, but not at the same time. Every morning Mary and Nanny cook fresh rolls that are yeasty and tender and the size of a large saucer. "People come here because they're tired of fast food," Mary said. "Do you know you can get one of our meals for about the same price as a hamburger and French fries at a fast-food place?" Good point. And you don't have to listen to some kid squawking unintelligibly over the drive-through speakers, either.

Jackson

Crechale's

3107 Highway 80 West
(601-355-1840)
Hours: Sunday-Thursday, 4:00 P.M.–
10:30 P.M.; Friday and Saturday,
4:00 P.M.–11:30 P.M.

When I called author Willie Morris to tell him I would be in Jackson, he offered to take me to one of his favorite eating places. The only hitch, he said, was that we might be accompanied by some

Howard R. Sanders (left), Willie Morris (center), and Gwen Sanders at Crechale's

of the Hollywood crew that was in town to film his book, *My Dog Skip*. Sure enough, two of the fellows from Hollywood arrived—David Bomba and Jay Russell–and Willie, his wife JoAnne, his son and daughter-in-law and a family friend trekked over to Crechale's, carrying our own liquor because of some strange Mississippi law or whatever. "You'll like Crechale's," Willie promised. "This is where Rob Reiner and the crew hung out while they were filming *Ghosts of Mississippi*. It's got a great juke-box that you can play for free." He proceeded to prove that claim once we were seated by playing enough Patsy Cline songs and other classics to last until the millennium. The restaurant, owned by Bob Crechale and managed by Juanita Jenkins, is comfortable and casual. The menu is a notch above the usual country cafe fare—fish and steaks—but there was a seafood platter and fried catfish available.

The conversation was convivial and interesting, the onion rings crisp and tasty once you dipped them in the "comeback sauce" (sometimes spelled kumback) a local, creamy garlic concoction that serves as a dipping sauce and a salad dressing, and the frog legs and flounder were fresh and delicious. The rolls were so hot and yeasty they would have been fine for a meal by themselves. In the midst of the meal, Willie wandered over to talk with an African-American couple, Howard R. Sanders, a school superintendent in a nearby county, and his wife Gwen, a former librarian, and I took the opportunity while he was gone to eat his share of the rolls. When we left an hour later toting Willie's leftover frog legs in a "froggy bag," Ray Charles was still going strong on the jukebox.

Mayflower Cafe

123 West Capitol Street
(601-355-4122)
Hours: Monday–Thursday, 7:30 A.M.–10:00 P.M.;
Friday and Saturday, 7:30 A.M.–11:00 P.M.

When I was looking for recommendations for restaurants in Mississippi, Howell Raines, the editorial page editor of *The New York Times*, enthusiastically endorsed the Mayflower. "I'm a great fan," Howell wrote. "Great redfish, great pompano, great steaks, and a fine tile floor."

He was right on all counts. The seafood at the Mayflower is superb, but so are the lunch specials of meat loaf, country-fried steak, veal cutlets, chicken and dumplings, and fried catfish. By noon,

Mike Kountouris, owner of the Mayflower Cafe

the place is packed with state-government workers, politicians, and others who know down-home cooking when they taste it. But I have to agree with Howell that the seafood is best of all. Fried catfish is great anytime, but if you want to tantalize your taste buds or impress your companion, get the Akropolis Special of broiled redfish with sautéed crabmeat, garnished with shrimp and oysters, and served with a special seafood sauce.

If this sounds Greek to you, you're right. Mike Kountouris has owned the Mayflower since 1935, and he hasn't forgotten his heritage. A short, friendly man in his eighties, Kountouris is also modest. I noticed a newspaper clipping and photograph that showed him embracing another man about his age. "That was a reunion a few years ago of some of us who fought in World War II," he said, and left it at that until I read the article and learned that he had been a volunteer in the Greek Battalion formed by Franklin Roosevelt to fight behind the Nazi lines in occupied Greece and blow up bridges and railroad tracks. Casualty rates were projected at ninety percent, yet Kountouris still volunteered. "Somebody had to do it," he explained simply. "I would do it again."

Two Sisters' Kitchen
707 North Congress
(601-353-1180)
Hours: Sunday-Friday, 11:00 P.M.–2:00 P.M.

Anybody who is eating over at the Mayflower Cafe apparently comes to the Two Sisters' Kitchen for lunch. The porch of the two-story house was crammed with people either leaving or arriving for the lunch buffet of fried chicken, chicken and dressing, peas, cabbage, corn, rice and gravy,

hot, fluffy yeast rolls, and iced tea as sweet as my waitress's Mississippi accent. As you enter the front door of Two Sisters', the buffet line is directly ahead on your left. Tell the greeter how many are in your party, and he'll send you to one of the dining rooms downstairs or upstairs. Grab a plate, fill it to a level just short of embarrassing, and find your table. The waitresses appear to refill your glass whenever your tea level dips below half full. Don't expect a quiet meal here. The throngs of people coming and going are friendly and boisterous. The vegetables are average, but the fried chicken is worth seconds and thirds.

Meridian

Jean's
2116 Front Street
(601-482-2348)
Hours: Monday-Friday, 6:30 A.M.–2:30 P.M.

Jean Bullock's cafe has been overshadowed by the reputation of Weidmann's, the famous restaurant just around the corner. Tourists go to Weidmann's, but locals seem to have a divided loyalty. Jean's was packed for lunch the day I was there, maybe because her prices are cheaper. For less than six dollars, you can get beef stew, spaghetti, chicken pot pie, chicken livers, or red beans and rice with sausage as an entrée, and a choice of three vegetables such as scalloped potatoes, stewed okra and tomatoes, baked squash, peas, or greens. The stewed okra and tomatoes were delicious, and the chicken pot pie had a nice flaky crust and lots of chicken. Nothing fancy here, just good, filling home-cooked food.

Weidmann's Restaurant

208 22nd Avenue
(601-693-1751)
Hours: Tuesday-Saturday, 7:00 A.M.–9:30 P.M.; Sunday and Monday, 7:00 A.M.–
    2:00 P.M.

Weidmann's is the place to eat in Meridian. Five generations of the family descended from Swiss immigrant Felix Weidmann have been running this dining establishment since 1870. For a time, Mississippi State All-American football player "Shorty" McWilliams ran the restaurant after he married one of the Weidmann daughters. Today, Shorty's daughter Gloria and her husband L.M. "Poo" Chancellor take care of the family business.

Gloria and L.M. "Poo" Chancellor, owners of Weidmann's

As you walk in the front door, you enter a high-ceilinged room with a brass-rail bar on one side and rows of tables against dark, aged paneling. The restaurant itself is steeped in history and filled with photographs of the famous and near-famous, from country-blues yodeler Jimmie Rodgers (a native son) and local football heroes to Babe Ruth and beauty queens.

The decor is fascinating, but the food is why people come here. And there is lots of it. The menu is so extensive it takes fifteen minutes to read. I've seen novels that weren't this long. One huge page is devoted to seafood alone, including red snapper, catfish, frog legs, oysters, rainbow trout, yellowfin tuna, scallops, and soft-shell crabs. You can't go wrong with any of the seafood. It's fresh and prepared with a light touch—

even the fried portions. The other side of the menu lists steaks, poultry, and specialties such as wiener schnitzel, calf liver, pork chops, corned-beef brisket with cabbage, parsley boiled potatoes, pickled beets and onions, and sliced tomatoes. And we haven't even gotten to the daily specials yet. The day I was there, I had to choose between salmon croquettes, oven-browned short-ribs with natural gravy and horseradish sauce, country-fried steak and brown mushroom gravy, homemade chicken pan pie, or fried crab cake. I closed my eyes and chose the short ribs, which were so tender the meat practically slid off the bone. The whole boiled potatoes and fried squash were perfect accompaniments, but I could have gotten field peas, yam soufflé, boiled baby okra, black-bing-cherry salad, steamed cabbage, or green beans. The rolls are light and wonderful, but you have to try the cracklin' cornbread. Southerners are familiar with it, but if you're from above the Mason-Dixon line, you need to know it's cornbread with bits of crisp fried pork fat blended in. Get a chunk of that with a bowl of greens and pot liquor, some sliced onions and tomatoes, and it's a cheap feast.

On the dessert list, just skip over the bread pudding (which is mighty buttery and tasty) and get the black-bottom pie. Weidmann's is known for this sinful dessert of a gingersnap crust topped with a chiffon of dark cocoa, flavored with just a touch of bourbon. Maybe you can talk your dining companions into ordering the egg custard or coconut custard pie, just for sharing.

Natchez

Mammy's Cupboard

555 Highway 61 South
(601-445-8957)
Hours: Tuesday–Saturday, 9:00 A.M.–4:00 P.M.

Mammy's Cupboard is a nightmare for the politically correct. Built by Henry Gaude in 1940, it is an architectural anachronism from past days. The restaurant is a towering replica of a woman with a long skirt and an apron, and a kerchief tied around her head. Originally, she was a black Mammy, but her features have been changed to make her appear more European. You still enter the restaurant under her skirt, though, which is another area of taste I won't get into. Before you browse through the gift shop, you can dine on daily hot lunches of chicken pot pie, red beans and rice, black beans, yellow rice, deviled-egg salad, cornbread, or angel biscuits. Otherwise, you can order sandwiches off the menu such as Mammy's Cupboard chicken-salad sandwich with pineapple and almonds or the sesame-chicken-salad sandwich on home-baked, whole-wheat bread. Everything is above average, especially the bread. You owe it to yourself to stop at Mammy's the next time you drive through Natchez. And bring a camera. A picture of your children in front of Mammy's will humiliate them the rest of their lives.

Ocean Springs

Aunt Jenny's Catfish Restaurant

1217 North Washington Avenue
(601-875-9201)
Hours: Tuesday-Thursday, 5:00 P.M.–9:00 P.M.; Friday and Saturday, 5:00 P.M.–
9:30 P.M.; Sunday, 11:30 A.M.–8:00 P.M.

To Native Americans living in the area before the white man came,
Ocean Springs was called "Holy Ground." Indians came from miles around
to drink from the springs that were considered magical. As white settlers
moved in, the town became a health resort. Riverboats brought visitors
by the thousands, guided through the bayou at night by torches that
were set on the bluff. One of the old waterfront houses from that era is
now Aunt Jenny's, where the curative powers of the spring water join
with the curative powers of the fried catfish. Aunt Jenny's makes no bones
about catering to tourists. There's a gift shop handy, a cellar lounge for
those who want more to drink than spring water, and a dining room that
features deliciously fried pond-raised catfish, fried chicken, shrimp, baked
yams, fried potatoes, and homemade biscuits. I recommend Kathy's batter-fried dill pickles, Paw-Paw's fried okra, Cousin Ray's onion rings, or
Talmadge's turnip greens as side dishes. The names may be cutesy, but
the food is plain good.

Oxford

Other Voices, Other Tastes

Ajax Diner

By Larry Brown

Photo courtesy of Algonquin Books of Chapel Hill

Ajax Diner is open from 11:30 A.M. until 10:00 P.M., and their telephone number is 601-232-8880. Drop by and see them any time. You'll be glad you did.

Ajax Diner sits on the west side of the square in Oxford, and although it's a new place, it's one of my favorites for lunch and dinner simply because the food is so good. This restaurant is the brainchild of City Grocery owner John Currence but is in the capable hands of manager Randy Yates, who is ready and willing to mix you a drink, serve you your salad, or get you some more napkins. Randy aims to please, and he does.

Randy offers lunch beginning at 11:30 A.M. with a good combination of items such as catfish, fried chicken, roast beef, pork chops, meat loaf, even chicken and dumplings. He has a wide array of vegetables, which are always fresh and tasty, and his cornbread is some of the best in town. I've found the service to be fast, efficient, and friendly. They have a large assortment of sandwiches ranging from fried oysters to barbecued pork and andouille sausage. Their burger is a big one, about eight ounces of beef served on Texas toast.

Some places know how to build a salad and some don't, but I always look forward to one from Ajax, the perfect beginning to a good meal. Ajax serves a vegetable plate for lunch as well, and it's always a popular item.

Through the big front windows you can see people walking on the square while you enjoy a drink or a beer. Ajax also offers soft drinks, coffee, hot or cold tea, and milk. It's a great place to take a kid for a meal.

Dinner at Ajax really shines, too. They don't take reservations, and even though the crowds are often large, there's plenty of seating available. Appetizers run the gamut from smoked-catfish dip served with tortilla chips to hot wings and boiled shrimp that are fat and ice cold. Their fried pickles are great, as well as their onion rings and the comeback sauce they serve with them.

All the sandwiches on the menu at lunch are available for dinner, with a choice of five salads. Dinner can assume a whole lot of forms at Ajax, including barbecued chicken, ribs, fried catfish, red beans and rice, grouper, pork loin, and a sixteen-ounce New York strip.

It just feels good to eat here. It's relaxed, it's not noisy, and you always know that whatever you order is going to be good. I've been eating here for the last few months, and I can honestly say that it's my favorite place in town to go with family and friends and spend a good evening. The zinc-topped bar up front is a good place to have a drink, and there are tall round tables just inside the door.

Larry Brown, a resident of Oxford, is the author of several acclaimed works of fiction, including the award-winning novel, *Father and Son*.

Onward

Other Voices, Other Tastes

The Booga Bottom Store

By Roy Blount

Photo by Louie Favorite

The Booga Bottom Store. I couldn't tell you how to get there, except that when you are heading north on Highway 61 in the Delta, you turn right on a one-lane blacktop. Somewhere. At Onward, Mississippi? Maybe. But I pick that only because it is such an extraordinary name for a town. A town named Onward is like a man named Anybody. A town named Onward, Mississippi, is like a man named Anybody N. Particular.

The Booga Bottom Store may not even be there for all I know. But Malcolm White of Jackson, Mississippi, took Slick Lawson, Greg Jaynes, and me there several years ago. For lunch. Booga Bottom used to be a plantation. The Booga Bottom Store was where the field hands ate. Fried chicken, chicken and dumplings, ham, cornbread, biscuits, and eight or ten good vegetables. Family style. The table was loaded. We ate like field hands.

Our waitress was named Hurdacine. She was hospitable, in a matter-of-fact way, as if hospitality came as naturally to her, and to everyone she knew, as her name did. "Eat up," she said, and we did.

Roy Blount, a native of Decatur, Georgia, is the author of a memoir, *Be Sweet*, a poem about grits, and several other books. He lives in New York.

Stoneville

Cicero's
Old Leland Road
(601-334-3315)
Hours: Monday-Friday, 11:00 A.M.–2:00 P.M and 5:00 P.M–10:00 P.M.; Saturday,
    5:00 P.M.–10:00 P.M.

Cicero's is hard to find (after driving north of Greenville about four miles on Highway 82, stop in Leland and ask directions. You'll probably have to do this two or three times.)

Acclaimed by *Mississippi* magazine and *Southern Living*, among others, Cicero's is a tiny place next door to the post office in Stoneville. As you walk inside, there's an old-fashioned meat cooler and display case to your left with the menu posted and the night's selection of fresh-cut filets and rib-eyes stacked in orderly rows. Lunch is pretty much a sandwich deal, the waitress said, since most of the customers

The meat cooler and display case at Cicero's

work for the agricultural chemical companies or other big farm businesses in the area and want something quick. If you're only there for lunch, I recommend the chopped barbecue-pork sandwich or the oyster po' boy. One of the house specialties is tamales, which you can get for $4.25 a half-dozen.

At night the place comes alive with folks eating steak, shrimp, catfish, oysters, corn fritters, fried dill pickles, or fried okra. If you're really hungry, try the Cat and Cow special. No, it's nothing like that. You get a choice of two from the shrimp, catfish, and steak dishes. Another thing. Cicero's may be out in the country, but some of their menu items are pretty fancy for farm folks. For example, who would have thought you could get a side order of shitake or portobella mushrooms in Stoneville, Mississippi?

Vicksburg

One of Walnut Hills's round tables

Walnut Hills Restaurant and Roundtable
1214 Adams Street
(601-638-4910)
Hours: Monday-Friday, 11:00 A.M.–9:00 P.M; Sunday, 11:00 A.M.–2:00 P.M.

This nineteenth-century house (it was built in 1880) sits in the heart of a city that was of strategic importance in the Civil War. The home of

Confederate president Jefferson Davis, Vicksburg surrendered to the Union army after months of fighting and forty-seven days of siege. If Walnut Hill and its roundtable dinners had been around in 1863, the Northern invaders probably would never have left. Instead, they have returned in droves as tourists to eat family style with their Southern cousins at one of the round tables.

Daily specials change at Walnut Hills, but you can always count on having fried chicken on the menu. For well under ten dollars you can partake of the chicken, spaghetti and meatballs, rice and gravy, purple-hull peas, eggplant casserole, green beans, mustard greens, okra and to-matoes, and bread pudding. If you sit at one of the round tables with the large lazy susan, you can spin and eat from any of the dishes served family style. Non-round tables are available for the less sociable. The fried chicken is some of the best you will taste and the bread pudding compares with that of the finest restaurants in New Orleans.

NORTH CAROLINA

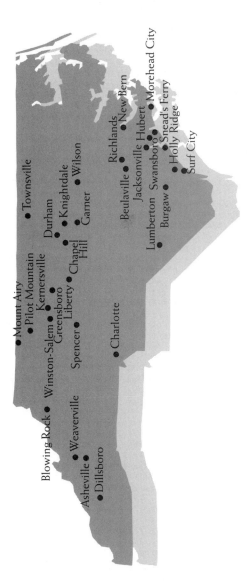

Morehead City
New Bern
Richlands
Hubert
Snead's Ferry
Beulaville
Jacksonville Swansboro
Holly Ridge
Surf City
Townsville
Lumberton
Burgaw
Wilson
Knightdale
Durham
Garner
Chapel
Hill
Mount Airy
Pilot Mountain
Kernersville
Greensboro
Winston-Salem Liberty
Spencer
Charlotte
Blowing Rock
Weaverville
Asheville
Dillsboro

Asheville

Moose Cafe

570 Brevard Road at the Farmer's Market
(828-255-0920)
Hours: Monday-Saturday, 7:00 A.M.–9:00 P.M.; Sunday, 7:00 A.M.–8:00 P.M.

Some cafe owners' idea of fresh vegetables is freshly opened canned green beans. You won't find any of that at the Moose Cafe, which is a corn muffin's throw away from the Asheville Farmer's Market. The only moose you'll find here is on the sign out front. Owners Bill and Margaret Walker say the restaurant is named after a previous proprietor, whose nickname was "Moose." No matter how it got its name, the Moose Cafe is a vegetarian's delight. With real mashed potatoes, fresh steamed cabbage, country-style collards, green beans, homemade potato salad, glazed carrots, and pinto beans on the menu, you might be tempted to forget about the meat

and get a vegetable plate. That would be unfortunate because then you would miss the Southern fried chicken, homemade meat loaf, country-style steak, country ham, and smoked pork chops. And don't skip the banana pudding. You can always diet tomorrow.

Beulaville

The Wagon Wheel

N.C. Highway 111 off of N.C. 24 East

(910-298-4272)

Hours: Wednesdays-Thursdays, 10:30 A.M.–8:00 P.M.; Fridays and Saturdays,
10:30 A.M.–9:00 P.M.; Sundays, 11:00 A.M.–2:30 P.M.

Collards is a Southern dish that either you like or you don't. Few of us are crazy about their aroma while cooking, but those who have never gotten past the smell don't know what they're missing.

Maybe the collard capital of the South is a restaurant in a little town near Charlotte. Once a week, The Wagon Wheel has Collard Day, and once a week the word goes out and throngs magically appear. *Charlotte Observer* food editor Kathleen Purvis, who has been an eyewitness to this phenomenon, reports that the spectacle is almost like a holy pilgrimage. "A couple of things you'll notice right away," Purvis says. "The crowd at the Wagon Wheel's Weekly Collard Day is not exactly young. This is a generation that calls the noon meal 'dinner.' And they dress up for it. Ladies (no other word will do) wear flowered dresses and lace collars and guardian-angel pins on their shoulders. Men wear short-sleeve cotton shirts and ties."

Of course, they don't just come for the collards, Purvis says. There's the backbone, too. Tender chunks of pork cooked so tender it slides off the bone. And there's more. A buffet of roast chicken, dumplings, fried chicken, mashed potatoes, gravy with bits of country-fried steak in it, fried fish, stewed potatoes, lima beans, hush puppies, sweet potatoes, and a salad bar. Owner Bo Carpenter estimates that he serves up to six hundred people on Tuesdays for dinner and supper. Collard Day, which used to be on Tuesdays, is now on Wednesdays. The master-collard chef is Carpenter's mother-in-law, Zannie Atkinson, who learned to cook at her mother's side when she was nine. Cooking the collards is almost as labor-intensive and time-consuming as barbecuing a pig. Once the best collards are rounded up and washed three or four times to get the sand out, they're cooked slowly overnight with seasonings. Purvis says Carpenter won't reveal the secret seasonings, but one customer pointed out that cabbage is cooked separately, chopped fine, and mixed with the collards. Whatever they do, no one's complaining. They just keep coming back for more.

Blowing Rock

Other Voices, Other Tastes
Sonny's Grill
By Jan Karon

While the store fronts on Blowing Rock's Main Street get more chic every season, Sonny's Grill looks just like it used to. The screen door is original, the geraniums in the window appear to be original, and all the fixtures are original, including Sonny Klutz. He's worked at the grill for forty-four years and knows exactly how his loyal customers like their livermush, hot dogs, cheeseburgers, and ham biscuits.

Sonny's contains six counter stools and four tables. In tourist season (which, dadgummit, is getting to be year-round), don't expect to find a seat for lunch. It's best to go for breakfast, before the tourists wake up. No later than seven o'clock, but six A.M. would be better.

Most of the regulars will be smoking, and the ancient geraniums will be wheezing, so what's the big attraction? Is it the food? Not exactly. Is it the place? Sort of. Is it Sonny? His cronies would say that's arguable. Is it the characters? There's a thought . . . .

In my opinion, it's the way the above ingredients fall together. In fact, Sonny's Grill is so like the small-town eating places we all knew as a child, it inspired the Main Street Grill in my four Mitford novels. So, just go. And tell Sonny I sent you.

Jan Karon is a Blowing Rock resident and author of *These High Green Hills* and other Mitford novels.

Burgaw

Holland's Shelter Creek Restaurant

7½ miles from Burgaw on Highway 53 East
(910-259-5743)
Hours: Sunday, 11:30 A.M.–9:00 P.M.; Monday and Tuesday, 11:00 A.M.–3:00 P.M.;
   Wednesday and Thursday, 11:00 A.M.–9:00 P.M; Friday and Saturday, 11:00 A.M.–
   10:00 P.M.

The first thing you notice when you walk into this rustic building at the entrance to a campground is the wooden Indian at the door. The second thing you notice is the stuffed black bear inside the store where all the hunting and fishing equipment is for sale. Take a right and you're in the restaurant overlooking Shelter Creek. Holland's Shelter Creek Restaurant serves seafood with a Cajun flavor. There's even a platter called Cajun Madness that features catfish and frog legs with your choice of shrimp creole or catfish stew. I'm not usually a big fan of catfish stew, but this was nice and spicy. The platter is $12.75; the stew alone is $6.95 and is served with hush puppies and choice of French fries, coleslaw, or applesauce. For those in the mood for sandwiches, Holland's has burgers, catfish, or oyster po' boys, pork chops, and bologna.

The wooden Indian that greets you at the door to Holland's Shelter Creek Restaurant

Chapel Hill

Mama Dip's Kitchen

405 West Rosemary Street
(919-942-5837)
Hours: Monday-Friday, 8:00 A.M.–3:00 P.M. and 4:00 P.M.–10:00 P.M.; Saturday,
   8:00 A.M.–10:00 P.M.; Sunday, 8:00 A.M.–9:00 P.M.

They call Mildred Council "Mama Dip" because the six-foot-tall lady has to "dip down" to serve food to her customers. After twenty-one years in the business, however, she spends more time in the kitchen than she does in the dining room of this local meat-and-veggie favorite that's only a couple of blocks from the University of North Carolina campus. Although it's a little pricier than some other down-home restaurants, Mama Dip's serves healthy portions of meat loaf, chicken salad, fried chicken, salmon patties, and two vegetables for six or seven dollars. The day I visited, UNC professor John Shelton Reed, author of several books on the South with such great titles as *My Tears Spoiled My Aim*, took time out to join me for lunch. John ordered sparingly—turnip greens and okra—in order to save room for what he described as a killer sweet-potato pie. I tried the salmon patty, squash casserole, and fried okra and wasn't disappointed. John made a wise choice with the sweet-potato pie and vanilla ice cream. I sampled a couple of bites and found it very custardy and delicious.

Later, Mildred Council explained how she had started the restaurant on little more than faith, friends, and sixty-

*Mildred Council (Mama Dip)
with John Shelton Reed*

two dollars. "I took the money and went to the grocery store to buy some eggs, bacon, grits, and bread for breakfast that first day," she said. "If somebody had paid with a twenty-dollar bill, I wouldn't have been able to change it." After collecting from her customers for breakfast, she trekked to the grocery store once more to buy pork chops and ground chuck and some vegetables for lunch. A story about the restaurant in the local paper brought more customers, including a group of hippies who lived nearby. "They dressed funny, but they were real nice," she said. "They'd come in and some would have money and some wouldn't. Now they still come in, but they're wearing suits and they've gotten married and have families."

Mama Dip cooks her food the way she learned as a child. "I was raised on vegetables during the Depression, that's why I have so many on the menu. I season my pintos, blackeyes, string beans, and greens with pork, but for everything else I use margarine." Despite the array of entrées every day, fried chicken is still everybody's favorite, she said.

She gets her vegetables from the Farmer's Market or from friends who bring in produce from their gardens during the summer. "I shell my own pecans, too. I buy three-hundred pounds at a time and whenever I'm sitting down back in the kitchen, I crack pecans. I guess I could buy them already shelled, but I enjoy doing it."

Charlotte

The Coffee Cup
914 South Clarkson Street
(704-375-8855)
Hours: Monday-Friday, 6:00 A.M.–3:00 P.M.; Saturday, 6:00 A.M.–noon.

By Jim Auchmutey

The Coffee Cup is more than a tasty little meat-and-three cafe in the shadow of downtown Charlotte. It's a monument to the biracial roots of Southern cooking.

Not that there's anything monumental-looking about the place. It sits across from a garage in a neighborhood of warehouses and trucking firms, a modest cinder-block building marked by a rusty old sign shaped like a coffee cup. Inside, there's a counter with eight ripped stools, ten brown Formica-topped tables, and a battered Rock-ola jukebox stocked with vintage soul. Which is pretty much what the kitchen is stocked with, too. The Coffee Cup's clientele, which ranges from businesswomen in tailored suits to mechanics with names stitched across their chests, feasts on plate lunches of fried chicken, collard greens, black-eyed peas,

Chris Crowder, owner of The Coffee Cup

and cobblers washed down with sweaty glasses of iced tea. They've even been known to nibble a pig's foot or two.

What makes the Coffee Cup special isn't just its authentically funky look or its genuine down-home food. It's the story behind them. When the cafe opened in the '40s, it was white-owned and only whites could take a seat. Black customers had to order take-out from a window that's still there, covered in plywood behind the cash register.

In the early '80s, the restaurant was sold to a couple of its waitresses—one black, one white—who tutored each other on the subtle differences between the way black and white Southerners cook. That's why the Coffee Cup today serves not only rib-sticking soul food but a good smattering of casseroles like you'd find at a white church supper. Customers of both races like both kinds of food. And so does the owner, a sassy black woman named Chris Crowder, who has run the restaurant since her former waitressing colleague, Mary Lou Maynor, died a few years ago. To Chris, those casseroles are more than menu items; they're a memorial to her white partner.

—*Jim Auchmutey is a reporter for* The Atlanta Journal-Constitution.

Dillsboro

Jarrett House

Intersection of U.S. 23 and U.S. 441 South
(828-772-2616)
Hours: Monday-Sunday, 7:00 A.M.–9:30 P.M.; 11:30 A.M.–2:00 P.M.; 5:00 P.M.–
8:30 P.M.

In earlier times, this three-story 1884 house was an inn where weary travelers could get a bed for themselves for a quarter and a meal for another dime. One of the owners is rumored to have made whiskey as well as cured hams there. Today, new owners Jim and Jean Harbarger have turned the house into a showplace with Victorian antiques and art work, and the only whiskey you'll find on the premises is that which customers tote in in brown bags. You will find cured ham, fried chicken, and other wonderful Southern food. For lunch, you have a choice of cured ham, baked ham, catfish, chicken and dumplings, or Southern fried chicken with coleslaw, candied apples, buttered potatoes, green beans, pickled beets, and hot biscuits. Dinner is basically the same, but with an additional choice of mountain trout, hand-battered and deep-fried. The biscuits are legendary, as is the peach cobbler, but I recommend you try the vinegar pie. Believe me, it tastes better than it sounds.

Durham

Bullock's Barbecue

3330 Quebec Street
(919-383-3211)
Hours: Tuesday-Saturday, 11:30 A.M.–8:00 P.M.

For a man who recently had heart-by-pass surgery, Tommy Bullock doesn't seem to be slowing down. He admits to working sixteen-hour days and neglecting his family just to maintain the forty-six-year reputation of his family's restaurant. When he's not on the phone taking catering orders, he's in the kitchen supervising the cooking or slicing a pineapple cake for dessert. Then there are the hours he spends slow-cooking the Eastern North Carolina-style barbecue.

"I'm just a compulsive personality," says Bullock, a rotund, earnest middle-aged man who calls everyone sir or ma'am. "I won't settle for something that's not right. And I make sure we serve quality food here. Everyone talks about our barbecue, but we have some of the best seafood you will find."

Tommy Bullock slices a pineapple cake.

Bullock is not exaggerating. The food here is so good that the television broadcast crews have Bullock's cater the press box whenever they're broadcasting ACC basketball games in the area. Hundreds of celebrities have stopped by and sampled Bullock's wares and left their signed pictures on the wall. On just one section, I saw Elvis and the Jordanaires, John Denver, Tony Orlando, Jeff Foxworthy, and Dolly Parton. Bullock says Oliver Stone ate here once when he was making a movie, but found no kitchen conspiracies.

If you're eating at Bullock's for the first time, you may want to do what I did and order a sampler plate of fried chicken, ribs, barbecue, green beans, Brunswick stew, coleslaw, French fries, and hush puppies. This is all-you-can-eat for $7.95. Otherwise, try one of the daily meat-and-three specials such as country-style steak and gravy, beef tips and rice, or spaghetti and meatballs, with fried okra, stewed corn, macaroni and cheese, turnip greens, or butter beans. Everything is fresh and first-rate, especially the banana pudding and pineapple cake.

Garner

Toot-N-Tell

903 Garner Road
(919-772-2616)
Hours: Monday-Saturday, 5:30 A.M.–9:00 P.M.; Sunday, 7:00 A.M.–3:00 P.M.

The Toot-N-Tell started in 1946 as a drive-in restaurant called the Toot-N-Tell It. There were no seats inside, just carhops who would bring your order to you. A few years later, seats were added and a drive-in window installed. In 1968, Bill and Mary Ann Sparkman bought the restaurant and continued to make improvements, including seven additions. The restaurant still has a drive-in window, but most people come inside now to fill up on one of the most amazing buffets I've seen. Maybe it's just because they had fried salt pork (or fried streak-o-lean), fried chicken, fried shrimp, barbecued ribs, fried fish, and yummy chicken and dumplings. Even after filling my plate with a sampling of each (all right, I got a bowl for the chicken and dumplings, or chicken and pastry, as they call it in North Carolina), I had room for some rutabagas, field peas, scalloped tomatoes, cabbage, mashed potatoes, and lima beans. I also dished up a spoonful of some chopped meat that was chewy and slightly vinegary. After a few mouthfuls (it wasn't bad; it tasted a little like clams), I asked the waitress what it was. She gave me an odd look and said "Chitterlings." Sorry I asked. Well, they were still tasty, although I didn't go back for second helpings of the pig intestines. I did return for more fried salt pork and chicken. After I had finished my meal, topped off with banana pudding and peach cobbler, I asked owner and cook Mary Ann Sparkman about the salt pork and chitterlings. I mean, these aren't the sort of things one usually finds on a Sunday buffet.

Mary Ann Sparkman, owner of the Toot-N-Tell

"Both are real popular," Mary Ann said. "But I guess the salt pork is the most popular. We fry five hundred pounds a week. People can't get enough of it."

I didn't tell her I had three servings along with four hush puppies. And I'm certainly not going to tell my doctor.

You can also order from the menu, which features burgers and sandwiches, seafood, and home-cooked meals such as chicken livers, chicken gizzards, pork chops, grilled calf liver with onions, country-style steak, chuck-wagon steak, and hamburger steak with onions and gravy. Even more bad news for my doctor.

Greensboro

Robinson's Restaurant
438 Battleground Avenue
(336-272-6854)
Hours: Monday-Friday, 6:30 A.M.–8:00 P.M.; Saturday, 6:30 A.M.– 3:00 P.M.

You would expect anyone named Roosevelt to be a Democrat, and

Roosevelt Robinson certainly is. Especially after Bill and Hillary Clinton, Al and Tipper Gore dropped in to eat during the 1992 campaign. The walls of the downtown restaurant are covered with photos of the Clintons and Gores and the Robinsons—Roosevelt and his wife, Freida—along with a thank-you note from Hillary Rodham Clinton. "Mrs. Clinton had some squash casserole and a slice of chocolate cake," Robinson said. "She said the cake was the best she ever ate." And Mr. Clinton? "He just had a cup of coffee," Robinson said, "but he was busy talking to everybody."

Well, Bill doesn't know what he missed. The food at Robinson's is delicious and freshly prepared by Freida herself. In addition to a full menu of seafood and steaks, Robinson's offers lunch specials with standard Southern delicacies such as squash casserole, chicken and dumplings, fried chicken, baked chicken, salmon patties, collard greens, and sweet-potato casserole. And Hillary was right. The squash casserole is really good. Add another vegetable and a meat and it's still a bargain for about four dollars. Or, if you're adventurous, try the special Salami Burger—a hamburger patty with salami and all the trimmings. Robinson said he concocted the sandwich one day when he was experimenting with what he had in the refrigerator. Customers liked it, and it stayed on the menu.

Roosevelt and Freida Robinson

Robinson's also serves breakfast for local businessmen and other regulars. And besides the usual bacon and sausage and biscuits, you can order fried bologna or scrambled brains and eggs.

Before opening the restaurant in 1977, Robinson worked in a bakery and was president of the baker's union. He credits his success with his wife's good cooking and a friendly atmosphere. "This is something my mama taught me," Robinson said. "Treat other people the way you want them to treat you."

Holly Ridge

Betty's SmokeHouse Restaurant

107 North Shore Drive
(910-328-0505)
Hours: Wednesday-Monday, 7:00 A.M.–9:00 P.M.

Betty's SmokeHouse Restaurant provides relief for those who have overdosed on seafood. Inside the barnlike, tin-roofed building, friendly waitresses quench your thirst with a giant glass of iced tea that requires two hands to handle and sate your hunger with eastern-style North Carolina barbecue, fried chicken, or other daily meat-and-three specials. The barbecue is vinegary and lean and perfect with or without the coleslaw, which, according to North Carolina tradition, is slathered on the bun with the meat.

Season to taste with Betty's own sauces. Whatever you get, however, let me suggest you order the collards. I don't know what magic was performed in the kitchen, but these were some of the tastiest, tenderest, sweetest greens I have eaten. The potato salad was creamy and delicious, with a touch of onions and pickles. Other vegetables include butter beans and corn, fried okra, green beans, macaroni salad, and coleslaw. Barbecue ribs and pork (chopped or sliced) are available anytime. Dinner is geared toward seafood and features a humongous seafood platter for two for less than twenty-five dollars.

Hubert

Bear Creek Cafe

419 Bear Creek Road
(910-326-4786)
Hours: Tuesday-Friday, 8:30 A.M.–9:00 P.M.; Saturday, 7:00 A.M.–9:00 P.M.; Sunday,
8:00 A.M.–3:00 P.M.

You really have to want to eat at Bear Creek Cafe to find it. The restaurant is about a mile from the main gate to Camp Lejeune off of Highway 172. If you can't find it, stop and ask the sheriff like I did. He gave me one of those looks that said, "You're not from around here, are you?" and then graciously gave me directions. Bear Creek Cafe owner Phyllis Manning serves everything from seafood to daily specials such as hamburger steak, pork loin, and beef stew. Vegetables include rutabagas, green beans, homemade potato salad, and cinnamon apples. The apples were particularly good, but probably the best thing on the menu is Phyllis' clam chowder, for which she has won several culinary prizes. Local, at least. She wouldn't give me the secret, but it's made with a cream base, and the seasoning was nearly perfect.

If you get to Bear Creek before lunch, don't worry. The breakfast is great, especially the biscuits and sausage gravy and the silver-dollar pancakes.

Jacksonville

Baker's Restaurant

3257 Richlands Highway
(910-346-6557)
Hours: Monday-Friday, 5:30 A.M.–8:30 P.M.; Saturday, 8:30 A.M.–11:30 A.M.

Baker's Restaurant has been an institution for decades in Jacksonville. After the previous owner died, Danny and Wanda Baysden bought the place in 1984 and continued to serve the meals that had become popular. This is real home-cooking. If you drop in on a Tuesday, I recommend you have the pork backbone with collards and butter beans. Top it off with some of the best banana pudding you'll ever taste, and you've got a pretty good meal. Other daily entrées include ham hocks, country-style steak, fried chicken, liver and onions, turkey and dressing, and fried pork chops. Like most good country restaurants, most of the budget is allocated for food and not in-

Wanda Baysden (right) and her daughter, Michelle Williford

terior decorating. "The regulars don't mind," Wanda said. "The same people come in here every day, sometimes twice a day. They like things the way they've always been, especially the food."

Kernersville

Donna Papasimakis, co-owner of Suzie's Diner

Suzie's Diner

Business 40 and Highway 66 South
(336-993-3313)
Hours: Sunday-Thursday, 5:00 A.M.–midnight; Friday and Saturday, twenty-four hours.

Suzie's Diner has been around for thirty-eight years, but after the original owner, Suzie Bodenheimer, died, the restaurant had a string of unsuccessful owners. For the past eight years, however, Gus and Donna Papasimakis have restored Suzie's reputation with a full diner-type menu of burgers and hot dogs and seafood and daily specials such as pot roast, roast pork, pork chops, country steak, fried chicken, liver and onions,

and meat loaf, with mashed potatoes, pinto beans, spinach, broccoli, cabbage, corn, and sweet potatoes.

Desserts are quite good, especially the buttermilk pie and baklava, but the best surprise was finding that the French fries were actually hand-cut and not frozen.

Owner Donna Papasimakis doesn't mind serving lots of Southern dishes, but when it comes to her personal choices, she opts for grilled chicken or eggplant parmesan. "I serve beans, but I don't like them," she said. "I'm Greek, and I was raised on beans. Beans, beans, beans. That's why I eat anything but beans."

Knightdale

Knightdale Seafood & BBQ

7201 Highway 64 East
(919-266-4447)
Hours: Monday-Saturday, 11:00 A.M.–9:00 P.M.; Sunday, 11:00 A.M.–8:00 P.M.

You know you have stumbled onto a good place to eat when the parking lot is almost full on a Saturday afternoon, and it's not even five o'clock yet. Shortly after I walked into Knightdale Seafood & BBQ, I saw why. It was all-you-can-eat, steak-and-shrimp night, and families with small children, elderly couples with matching walkers, and middle-aged married couples out for a night on the town were crowded around tables laden with platters of hush puppies, seafood, barbecue, and steak. Other specials on the blackboard were trout, perch, trigger fish, and T-bone steaks.

Knightdale's is the kind of place where you can close your eyes, point to the menu, and not go wrong. If you're in the mood for barbecue, they serve that family-style, chopped or sliced, with fried chicken, coleslaw, boiled potatoes, string beans, Brunswick stew, and hush puppies. And you can add any seafood except jumbo shrimp for $1.75 extra.

While you're waiting for an order off the menu (I tried the steak and shrimp), the waitress brings a bowl of complimentary hush puppies in the size and shape of slightly crooked index fingers. They were sweet and light and delicious. Then she brings you your own pitcher of sweet tea and a bowl of ice. The sign over the double doors to the kitchen reads "Dale Earnhardt Dr." It's appropriate, because these waitresses hustle in and out faster than a lot of NASCAR drivers. I barely had a chance to survey the paintings and old posters of Sir Walter Raleigh tobacco and Greyhound bus lines when my food arrived. Everything was sinfully good. I only regret I didn't look at the menu more carefully before I ordered. Otherwise I would have gotten the baked sweet potato instead of the baked Irish potato. I know that's sacrilege for someone named O'Briant, but it's hard to find baked sweet potatoes in restaurants.

All the hustle of the staff had its effect. I was out of there in less than forty-five minutes, and by then the line had already formed on the front porch.

Liberty

Fran's Front Porch
6139 Smithwood Road
(336-685-4104)
Hours: Thursday–Saturday, 5:00 P.M.–8:30 P.M.; Sunday, noon–2:30 P.M.

Fran's Front Porch is a down-home buffet served in a wonderful historic house in the middle of nowhere. Actually, it's a few miles from Liberty, which is south of Greensboro. The 1911 house with the wraparound porch is where Fran Holt was born. In 1976, she and her daughters Sylvia and Carolyn decided to open a restaurant and held a yard sale to finance the operation. Featured in Dawn O'Brien's book, *North Carolina's Historic Restaurants and Their Recipes*, Fran's serves up scrumptious chicken pot pie and a squash casserole that is cheesy and delicious. The restaurant is known for its lemon chess pie, but I wouldn't pass up the chocolate cream pie, either.

Lumberton

Other Voices, Other Tastes

Fuller's

By Josephine Humphreys

As it nears Lumberton, Interstate 95 breaks out in an angry rash of billboards and motels, and traffic slows to a single creeping lane. By my reckoning this stretch of road has been under repair for the last ten years, which is about how long I've been driving it in order to get to my favorite restaurant, Fuller's, at Exit 20.

But I'll endure anything to get to Fuller's. I've been known to hop in the car and drive non-stop, pick up six dinners to go, and drive back home in time to feed the family an almost-hot meal. And that's an accomplishment. It's a long drive. About three hundred miles round trip, Charleston to Lumberton and back.

But when I can, I'd rather eat in than take out. I like the reserved friendliness of Fuller's; I feel welcome but not fussed-over. It's a dignified place, family-run, with a never-ending buffet of beans (three kinds), rice, chopped pork, collards, cabbage, sweet potatoes, ribs, chicken, and more—everything home-grown and home-cooked but better than anything my home ever produced. The pork is the way I like it, chopped fine with a hint of peppery vinegar, no mustard, no ketchup. Fuller's has the best chicken gizzards I've ever eaten—the *only* chicken gizzards I've ever eaten—fried so light and airy that the gristly crunch of gizzard is positively heavenly. (I swear.) And on Sundays the oysters! And scallops, shrimp, chicken livers, fresh and golden-fried, all you can eat. Oh, and the blood sausage!

I'll tell you, though, even if Fuller's didn't serve the best food in the South, it might still be my favorite restaurant. On any given day (except December 25, when it's closed) you will see a rainbow coalition eating in Fuller's, maybe a wider variety than you're used to because Fuller's draws customers from all over. Even Yankees, off the interstate. Food unites. What's more, Fuller's is located in the heart of Lumbee Indian territory. It's Lumbee-owned, and a Lumbee gathering spot.

Fuller and Delora Locklear both come from old Lumbee families, and a good bit of their history is documented on the walls of the restaurant, in photographs and paintings, farm implements, Native American art. The great outlaw Henry Berry Lowry looks down upon one corner of the room, and I always try to sit within range of his brooding gaze. There are usually Locklear children and grandchildren around, and other members of the Lumbee community.

"Fuller was farming," Dee Locklear says, remembering how they got started. "And I was working at the plant, and the farming got bad. We couldn't pay our bills. He was cooking the meat anyway, for schools and churches, and he said we might as well open a restaurant. And we've done well. Better than I ever, ever, thought we would."

The specialties most typically Lumbee are chicken and pastry ("pastry" meaning wide home-rolled noodles), and a round, flat, delicious cornbread similar to the Indian frybread of other tribes but not quite the same. Dee's sister-in-law Bonnie says, "It's not many restaurants that will take the time to hand-fry cornbread, each single piece. That was Fuller's idea. He insisted on it, he didn't care how much trouble it was. The restaurant was *going* to have fried cornbread."

Reynolds Price is a fan of Fuller's. He says he was tempted by the fatback but passed it up. I, on the other hand, have never passed it up. It's the best fatback I've ever eaten (and yes, the *only*) crispy and bacony and so tasty it *can't* be bad for me . . . and anyway I balance it with an extra helping of greens (the only greens I've ever really loved, with no hint of the bitter taste they always have at home) and then some more sweet corn, and black-eyed peas, and limas . . . .

Josephine Humphreys is the author of *Rich in Love* and other novels. She lives in Charleston, South Carolina.

Morehead City

Cox Family Restaurant

4109 Arendell
(252-726-6961)
Hours: Monday-Sunday, 6:00 A.M.–9:00 P.M.

I know one shouldn't judge a restaurant by its waitresses, but sometimes the age and disposition of the servers indicate how good the food will be. If the waitress has big hair, has been a member of AARP for at least a decade, and is named Maxine or Eulene, get ready for some good eating. My waitress was a grandmotherly type named Maxine Taylor who hovered over me like my own grandmother used to, refilling my coffee cup, asking how everything was. Everything was just fine. Maybe that's why Ray Cox and his sister Faye Collins have been in business here for twenty-one years. Considering the life span of restaurants, that's a remarkable record. Almost as remarkable as their hotcakes. Two of these come with one egg and two slices of bacon and are about the size of a salad bowl. Slather a couple of pats of butter between them, add a generous dollop of syrup, wash it down with a tall glass of milk and you've loaded up enough carbohydrates to run the Boston Marathon. Twice. In spite of their size, these hotcakes are light and delicious. For even more calories, try Mike's Chocolate Chip hotcakes or a side orders of biscuits with sausage gravy.

Lunch is even more amazing. In addition to daily entrées such as fried chicken, chicken and pastry, beef tips, or seafood, the restaurant offers a choice of two vegetables from a list of fifteen or more. Drop in on the right day and you can have fresh turnip roots, dried butter beans, fried cabbage, fried okra, mashed potatoes, or pickled beets. Prices are less than four dollars and include dessert. I recommend the lemon pie. But not after you've had a couple of those hotcakes.

Mount Airy

The Derby Restaurant

Intersection of Business 52 and Highway 89
(336-786-7082)
Hours: Tuesday-Saturday, 7:00 A.M.–8:00 P.M.; Sunday, 7:00 A.M.–7:00 P.M.

The Derby is Surry County's oldest full-service restaurant. For fifty years, three generations of the Pell family have been serving breakfast, lunch, and dinner specials. Breakfast features biscuits made from scratch, fried tenderloin, and pork brains and eggs as well as the usual bacon, sausage, and ham. For slightly more than four dollars, you can get a lunch special of one meat and three vegetables from a list that includes country-style steak, baked ham, hamburger steak with gravy and onions, and other meats, and white beans, collards, candied yams, potato salad, pinto beans, boiled cabbage, and buttered corn. Fried squash, by the way, is one of the restaurant's specialties. Tuesday and Wednesday nights are all-you-can-eat flounder nights, and Thursday night is spaghetti.

The Snappy Lunch

125 North Main Street
(336-786-4310)
Hours: Monday, Tuesday, Wednesday, Friday, 5:45 A.M.–1:45 P.M.; Thursday and
    Saturday, 5:45 A.M.–1:15 P.M.

Mount Airy's claim to fame, besides being a picturesque foothills village, is the fact that it's the model for Andy Griffith's Mayberry on television. Thousands of fans pour into the town every September for Mayberry Days. And one of the main attractions any time of the year is the Snappy Lunch, home of the world-famous pork-chop sandwich. The little storefront diner was mentioned in an early episode of *The Andy Griffith Show* entitled "Andy the Matchmaker" when Andy suggested to Barney that they go to the Snappy Lunch to get a bite to eat. He also mentioned the Snappy Lunch in his version of the song *Silhouettes*. In one interview, Griffith talked about getting a hot dog and a soft drink for fifteen

cents at the Snappy Lunch when he was a young boy. TV personalities, including Oprah Winfrey and Lou "The Incredible Hulk" Ferrigno, have visited the cafe.

Charles Dowell holds a pork chop, the key ingredient in the Snappy Lunch's pork-chop sandwich.

The Snappy Lunch was opened in 1923 by George Roberson and Deuce Hodge. Present owner Charles Dowell began working as a cook in 1943 and eventually bought out the proprietors. In those days, Dowell said, you could buy a hot dog for a dime or a bologna sandwich for a nickel. Now, pork-chop sandwiches account for more than ninety percent of the food sold, Dowell said. These are not your ordinary pork-chop sandwiches. Created by Dowell, these are salad-plate-size slices of loin chops that are tenderized by a special machine. Dowell then slow cooks a couple of dozen on a grill in the kitchen before bringing them out to brown on a higher-temperature grill in the front of the cafe in the storefront window in plain view of passersby. The finished product is put on a heated bun and covered with lettuce, tomato, chili, slaw, onions, mustard, and mayonnaise, and anything else you can think of.

There's no reason to get anything other than a pork-chop sandwich, but there are other things on the menu. Dowell's fried hot dogs with homemade chili are marvelous, and his burgers are hand-shaped and grilled to perfection. (You can get an all-meat patty or a patty mixed with bread crumbs, like your Mama used to make when she was trying to stretch the food budget).

New Bern

The Berne Restaurant
2900 Neuse Boulevard
(919-638-5296)
Hours: Monday-Thursday, 5:30 A.M.–8:00 P.M; Friday and Saturday, 5:30 A.M.–
   9:00 P.M.; Sunday, 5:30 A.M.–7:00 P.M.

Most of the restaurants in this picturesque, historic town are simply too fancy to fit in the down-home cooking category. For that, you have to drive a couple of miles out Broad Street to Neuse Boulevard and The Berne Restaurant. For thirty-five years, this large, functional restaurant has been the meeting place for the Kiwanis and other civic groups as well as regular customers who come here for the breakfast, lunch, and dinner buffets. If you want seafood, come on Friday for trout, catfish, shrimp, and a half-dozen different vegetables and a salad bar. Sunday is fried chicken, chicken and dressing, chicken and pastry (a North Carolina dish that resembles a pot pie with dumplings). I arrived on a Saturday and had a choice of barbecue, corned beef, and baked chicken, with cabbage, mashed potatoes, green beans, collards, coleslaw, and pickled beets. Being indecisive, I sampled them all. All right, I did go back for a second helping of barbecue. It's hard to get good barbecue on a buffet line, but this was not bad, especially if you add some of the vinegar-based sauce. If you're not in the mood for the buffet, menu items include a variety of seafood, steaks, hamburgers, chicken livers, beef liver, country-fried steak, and lasagna.

Pilot Mountain

Mountain View Restaurant
Pilot Mountain
(336-368-9180)
Hours: Monday-Saturday, 6:00 A.M.–9:00 P.M.; Sunday, 6:00 A.M.–2:00 P.M.

Breakfast is your best bet at Mountain View Restaurant, an established eating place that sits between a McDonald's and a motel. The biscuits are better than some of the fast-food variety, and you won't be able to get your eggs with bologna or tenderloin at the Golden Arches. If you're late for breakfast, Mountain View serves a serviceable buffet of popcorn shrimp, meat loaf, fried chicken, fried apples, collard greens, and macaroni and cheese.

Richlands

Arnold's Family Restaurant
Highway 258
(910-324-3278)
Hours: Monday-Thursday, 6:00 A.M.–11:00 P.M.; Friday and Saturday, 6:00 A.M.–
    midnight.

Arnold's combines the best of the old-fashioned drive-in burger joint (there is a drive-through) with a country buffet. If you're in the mood for the kind of burger you remember from your youth, try the Big-A Burger. It's juicy and hand-shaped and delicious. On the buffet, eat your fill for about five dollars. I recommend the fried chicken, but the stuffed peppers were good, too. Other entrées, depending on the day, include country steak, roast beef, beef stew, and meat loaf. Knotty-pine paneling creates a homey warmth in the back dining room. And afterward, stop by the ice-cream counter for a sundae or shake.

Snead's Ferry

Buddy's Restaurant
1974 Highway 172
(910-327-1357)
Hours: Monday-Sunday, 6:00 A.M.–10:00 P.M.

Snead's Ferry is named for Robert Snead, one of two men who owned ferries on the New River in the eighteenth century. The ferries were a key element on the Post Road linking Suffolk, Virginia, with Charleston, South Carolina, until a bridge was built in 1939.

Before you cross that bridge, however, it's worth your while to sample three pretty good restaurants in the area. Buddy's has the requisite seafood found in towns so close to the coast

(a platter of eight entrées is less than twenty dollars and will feed a half-dozen Marines from nearby Camp Lejeune), but the restaurant also has daily specials of pork chops, meat loaf, or other entrées. Choose two vegetables from corn, mashed potatoes, baked sweet potatoes, fried squash, macaroni and cheese, or peas. The pies are homemade and good, especially the coconut cream and the apple.

Clamdigger Family Restaurant

¼ mile from Four Corners on Highway 72
(910-327-3444)
Hours: Monday-Sunday, 5:30 A.M.–
    10:00 P.M

Got collards? Maybe it's just a co-incidence, but I did not have a bad serving of collards in North Carolina. The ones at Clamdigger's were as tasty as those at Betty's SmokeHouse. And they were the perfect complement to the fried pork chops. Clamdigger's is a relatively new restaurant that serves breakfast, lunch, and dinner buffets. Saturdays are for seafood when you can eat all you like of shrimp, fish, crab, and all of the accompaniments. Sunday is country-buffet time with chicken and pastry, roast beef, ham, and turkey. If you happen by in the early morning, I strongly urge you to try the breakfast buffet. Sure, you can get the country ham and biscuits if you like, but the strawberry waffle is my choice.

Riverview Cafe

119 Hall Point Road
(910-327-2011)
Hours: Sunday-Thursday, 11:00 A.M.–9:00 P.M.;
    Friday, 11:00 A.M.–9:30 P.M.; Saturday,
    11:00 A.M.–10:00 P.M.

It's worth stopping at the Riverview Cafe just for the view. Set on a bluff overlooking the New River, Johnny Terwilliger's restaurant is casual and comfortable with an intimate horseshoe-shaped bar that is usually filled with locals discussing North Carolina basketball, the economy, or the fishing. Basketball was the topic the day

I was in there, and pork chops was the special. They were fried golden brown and had no greasy taste, but the fried rock shrimp was even better. It was nice to have real fried okra that was not pre-battered and frozen, and the garlic cheese potatoes were wonderful. Other choices of vegetables include cabbage, peas, macaroni and cheese, fried squash, butter beans and corn mixed, and cucumber salad. The seafood platters are monstrous for around fifteen dollars.

Spencer

Ann's Cafe

319 Main Street
(704-633-3889)
Hours: Monday-Friday, lunch served from 11:00 A.M.–3:00 P.M.; dinner from
4:30 P.M.–7:00 P.M.

Ann and Buddy Poplin, owners of Ann's Cafe

You have to look hard to find Ann's Cafe, a tiny place tucked away in the corner of a shopping center. But all you have to do is ask anyone in town, and they can direct you there immediately. Opened for about a year, Ann's Cafe is owned by Ann and Buddy Poplin. Ann does the cooking, and Buddy does the talking. Both were in other businesses for years and decided they really wanted to have a restaurant. Ann brought family recipes that she learned from the time she was barely able to hang onto her grandmother's apron strings. "I've always loved to cook," she says. "I grew up in Washington, North Carolina, on the coast, and I used to stand on a stool in my grandmother's kitchen and help her."

Everything in Ann's is freshly prepared, from the fried squash, fried okra, and fried green tomatoes to the chicken and dumplings. Daily specials include country steak, pot roast, turkey and dressing, and vegetable plates. Highly recommended: any of the fried vegetables, the potato salad, the chicken and dumplings, the pot roast, and the carrot cake.

Surf City

The Crab Pot
Route 50 on the Causeway
(910-328-5001)
Hours: Monday-Sunday, 11:30 A.M.–10:00 P.M.

This Surf City is not what the Beach Boys had in mind when they recorded their hit song. But if the California group had ever visited this small town on the Intracoastal Waterway they probably would have eaten at The Crab Pot. The rustic restaurant is usually packed during the tourist season as much for the entertainment and drinks as for the fresh seafood. (A college student's dream is the sixty-four-ounce margarita). Along with the assortment of alcoholic beverages is a menu that features crabs by the half-dozen, shrimp, oysters, conch chowder, and she-crab soup. What's unusual about The Crab Pot's menu, however, are the side dishes. You have a choice of fried green tomatoes, fried turnip rings, dirty rice, white beans au gratin, red beans and rice, or Caribbean rice and peas. House specialties are the clam chowder, shrimp and creamy grits, or a steamer bucket of seafood known in North and South Carolina as Frogmore Stew. For around fifteen dollars you get crab legs, shrimp, clams, oysters, corn on the cob, kielbasa sausage, and potatoes. Not in the mood for seafood? Don't worry. One of the menu items is a fried bologna sandwich.

Unlike some Australian eating establishments, The Crab Pot does have rules. Rule No. 4: If you must sing, please refer to the Anderson Book of Etiquette as to the type of music best suited for an establishment specializing in fun, food, and drink. Selections such as songs by the Mormon Tabernacle Choir, a medley of James Brown tunes, and other compositions of a similar nature are preferred by the management.

Mollie's
107 North Shore Drive
(910-328-0505)
Hours: Wednesday-Monday, 7:00 A.M.–9:00 P.M.

Just up the street from The Crab Pot, Mollie's offers a calmer atmosphere and a good breakfast menu as well as down-home lunch specials that vary. Typical offerings include fried shrimp, stew beef, barbecue chicken, cabbage rolls, and tuna-stuffed tomatoes, along with a choice of two vegetables.

Wander in for dinner, however, and it's a different story. There's seafood galore, as fresh as possible and delicately fried. Mollie's has a very good breakfast with homemade biscuits, eggs, bacon, sausage, and grits. And for those who need a beef fix, there's a hamburger steak or a rib-eye steak breakfast.

Swansboro

T & W Oyster Bar Restaurant
3231 Highway 58
(252-393-8838)
Hours: Monday-Saturday, 5:00 A.M–10:00 P.M.; Sunday, noon–10:00 P.M.

I had heard many stories about T & W Oyster Bar before I actually saw it. Some folks said it had a tree growing in the middle of it. Others raved about the fresh oysters and shrimp.

Well, I have to say one of the stories was not true. I didn't see a tree growing up in the middle, although I did see two cedar poles with barely-trimmed limbs supporting the main dining room ceiling. And I'm happy to say the claims about the quality of the seafood were not exaggerated. The best way to eat at the T & W is to sit at one of the long bars, preferably in front of the fireplace in winter, and order a half-peck of the steamed oysters. In the past, my only complaint about steamed oysters was that I had to shuck them myself. Even at that wonderful South Carolina establishment, Bowen's Island, I had to surrender out of sheer exhaustion before I was completely satisfied. Not so at T & W. The bartenders ask you if you want your oysters barely steamed, moderately steamed, or dry, and then proceed to steam them to your specifications. While you're waiting, you can nibble on a basket of delicious hush puppies that are unusually shaped—they look like fat French fries—and sip on a frosty drink. Hot butter and cocktail sauce are poured into two compartments of a heavy-duty paper plate and your shucked oysters—that's right, they shuck them for you—are tossed into the third compartment much faster than you can eat them.

If you don't like oysters, and I feel sorry for you if you don't, there are scallops, crab legs, shrimp, trout, crabs, and flounder. Most everything comes either fried, steamed, or broiled. Prices range from about seven dollars for a senior-citizen shrimp platter to twenty-one dollars for a peck (a large bucket) of steamed oysters. While you're waiting, check out the hornets' nests on the cedar poles or talk to your fellow bar diners. I found them to be extremely friendly. One retired gentleman gave a testimonial to the freshness of the oysters (he was correct) and another fellow, a blue-collar worker waiting for a takeout, explained that steel was a solid business, and he would never worry about layoffs with his company.

Teddy Sweet (left) and Donald Jordan shuck oysters at T & W Oyster Bar Restaurant

Townsville

The Olde Place

Between the Townsville Volunteer Fire Department and the Episcopal Church on the west side of N.C. 39

(252-438-4770)

Hours: Wednesday-Friday, 5:00 P.M.–9:00 P.M.;Saturday and Sunday, 7:30 A.M.–1:00 P.M. and 5:00 P.M.–9:00 P.M.

By Jack Betts

No one can remember how long a restaurant has stood in the center of tiny Townsville, a village twelve miles north of Henderson on N.C. 39 near the Virginia border. Ralph Pegram figures at least fifty years, maybe more, though he and Marjorie Pegram have owned and operated The Olde Place restaurant for the last decade.

They, and their cooking, have become legends to thousands of bass fishermen who have eaten the huge, early-morning breakfast buffets (five dollars a head and all you can eat) that the Peagrams have laid out for years, and to thousands more sailors and skiers from nearby John H. Kerr Reservoir, who drop by in the evenings to gorge on the Pegram's country-cooking vegetable buffets for seven dollars.

Without the mammoth lake—55,000 surface acres and more than 800 miles of shoreline on the Roanoke River—The Olde Place might simply be an old place in the road in a sleepy little northern Piedmont town. Instead, it has a steady clientele of big eaters from places like Oxford, Warrenton, Henderson, and Clarksville, Virginia. This is still tobacco and textile country, and folks like their food hot, well done, and quick.

That's what you get at The Olde Place, starting with a cup or a bowl of the Pegram's memorable catfish chowder. It's worth ordering every time, and gives you a moment to figure out what you're going to eat. Count on this: a lot. Even those who just get the vegetable bar find themselves shoveling in a ton of food: deviled eggs, whipped sweet potatoes good enough to be dessert, hot apples, snap beans, cut corn, potato salad, mashed potatoes, turnip greens, and an assortment of rolls, biscuits, and hush puppies.

The entrées run like this: catfish plate, nine dollars for the small and eleven dollars for the large; fried chicken, six or eight dollars with the vegetable bar (without a doubt, The Olde Place's best deal for big-time eaters). The weekend specials are good. On Saturday, there's prime rib for twelve dollars (thirteen dollars with the vegetable bar) and half a barbecued chicken for $8.50. The chicken is superb.

Sandwiches are good. Our favorite, hands down, is the flounder sandwich with slaw and tartar sauce for three dollars. It comes with cheese, but it's better without. It's a big sandwich, hot and juicy, and they know how to do slaw and tartar sauce just right.

One of the quirky things folks like about The Olde Place is the prices include taxes. If you order the seven-dollar vegetable bar, that's what you pay—seven dollars. Ralph and Marjorie Pegram don't believe in complicating your life. They want to fill you up and see you coming back.

Make no mistake—it's the food that brings them back. The homey, rural atmosphere is not much of a draw, although regulars find its unpretentious ways and rural appointments charming in their own way. The front room has a short bar with stools and a few booths, usually occupied by regulars. The main part of the restaurant features a big fireplace at one end—with a hot fire blazing in winter—and a couple of dozen plywood-topped tables with ladder-back chairs. There's a front eating porch when the crowd gets heavy, and a meeting room tacked onto the side where civic clubs meet once a week. The decor, if that's the right word, runs to barn siding with some nautical prints and a couple of murals depicting rural scenes. Floors are concrete, the ice tea comes in Mason jars, and while you're waiting, Ralph Pegram will drop by to say howdy and repeat the jokes he's heard that week.

—*Jack Betts is the associate editor of the* Charlotte Observer.

Weaverville

Stoney Knob Restaurant

337 Merrimon Avenue
(828-645-3309)
Hours: Tuesday-Friday, 7:00 A.M.–6:00 P.M.; Saturday, 7:00 A.M.–3:00 P.M.; Sunday,
   8:00 A.M.–3:00 P.M.

If you're in the Asheville area, drive north about eight miles on U.S. Highway 25 to Weaverville and check out the Stoney Knob Restaurant, if for no other reason than to see the owners, John and Yotty Dermas. The Greek brothers are dead ringers for Elvis. In fact, if Elvis were still alive (I know, I know. You saw him at the Burger King last month), this is a place he would frequent. The daily specials include baked chicken

John Dermas (left) and Yotty
Dermas, owners of Stoney Knob
Restaurant

with dressing and country-style steak with rice and gravy, and a multitude of fresh vegetables, but I recommend the baked lamb shank with rice. "It was hard to get the local folks to try some of our Greek dishes at first," says John Dermas, "but now they call and ask us when we're having lamb shanks again." Breakfast is a popular meal, too, with hot cakes and feta-cheese omelettes.

Wilson

Mitchell's Chicken, Barbecue and Ribs Restaurant
6228 South Ward Boulevard
(252-291-9189)
Hours: Tuesday-Saturday, 10:30 A.M.–7:00 P.M.; Sunday, 10:30 A.M.–6:00 p.m.

If I hadn't gotten lost in Wilson and taken a wrong turn, I wouldn't have gone past Mitchell's. And if I hadn't gone by Mitchell's, I wouldn't have spotted the Harlem Globetrotters' bus parked out front. Forget the old wives' tale about truck drivers knowing the best places to eat. (Wrong, wrong, wrong. They stop where they have room to park their trucks, get fuel, and take showers.) If you want to know where the best food is, follow the Harlem Globetrotters' bus.

The outside of Mitchell's is kind of shabby, which is exactly the way a barbecue place is supposed to look. A separate cement-block building functions as the pit house, or the place where two huge covered grills are stoked constantly to slowly roast whole pigs overnight. After the pigs are done, the cooks add chickens, ribs, and pork chops.

My dream of meeting the Globetrotters vanished when the bus pulled away just as I parked. Inside the restaurant, the crowd was still buzzing. Several had seen the ball-handling exhibition the Globetrotters had put on the night before in town. "They didn't look that tall on the court last night," one customer said, "but they're TALL, man! And they could put away some food!" Owner Ed Mitchell said the players had eaten ribs, barbecue, macaroni and cheese, hush puppies, and greens from the buffet and were very complimentary. That's not surprising, especially after I tried the tender, juicy chopped-pork barbecue with vinegar sauce and a half-dozen ribs dipped in Mitchell's sweet-and-spicy tomato sauce. White beans, collard greens, hush puppies, and sweet-potato pie made the culinary experience almost orgasmic. The hush puppies were a mixture of corn meal and flour and were yeast-like in their sweet lightness. For non-barbecue lovers, Mitchell's offers fried chicken, steak, and pork chops along with a half-dozen vegetables.

After I ate, I learned that Mitchell was quite a celebrity. He was included in Bob Garner's book, *North Carolina Barbecue*, and was featured on the Public Broadcasting System's television documentary.

With no prodding at all, Mitchell offered to show me how the meat is cooked in the pit house. "Slow and careful," he says. "You can't rush it. It's very labor intensive."

Mitchell seems to be an unlikely barbecue entrepreneur. Born in Wilson County, he has a degree in sociology from Fayetteville State University and attended graduate school at East Carolina University. He has worked for the North Carolina Department of Labor, run his own real-estate and remodeling companies, and managed a Ford dealership. He was drawn to the smoky lure of barbecue in the early 1990s after his father died. Mitchell's parents had run a mom-and-pop grocery on the same site as the present restaurant for years. After Mitchell's father died in 1990, customers drifted away, and his mother became depressed.

One day, he walked in when she was feeling extremely low. To take her mind off her grief, he asked her what she was cooking. Greens, she said, then added that she really had a taste for barbecue. Mitchell went to the storage room, pulled out an old grill, and bought a thirty-four-pound pig at a local store. While they were eating a lunch of barbecue later in the store, a customer came in to buy a hot dog, noticed the pig cooking out back, and asked to buy a couple of barbecue sandwiches. They sold all of the barbecue that day, and Mitchell's mother was happy again. "I remember my mother saying that people were getting tired of fast food and wanted things like black-eyed peas, collards, and old-fashioned vegetables." As more customers came in during the next few days to ask for barbecue, Mitchell says he finally figured out they were onto something and remodeled the store as a restaurant.

The most satisfying part of the barbecue business, Mitchell says, is the camaraderie among all who dine there. "All races come in here and eat together, talk and enjoy the good old Southern atmosphere. All the titles and pedigrees are left at the door."

Winston-Salem

Bell & Sons Cafeteria

4320 North Liberty Street
336-767-0703
Hours: Monday-Saturday, 10:30 A.M.–8:00 P.M.; Sunday, 11:00 A.M.–3:00 P.M. and
4:30 P.M.–8:00 P.M.

The sign out front still says Bell Brothers Cafeteria, but the official name now is Bell & Sons, for owners James Bell and his sons Randy and Wayne. Don't go into this restaurant expecting a cookie-cutter version of Morrison's Cafeteria. While some dishes on the lineup may seem similar, the taste is definitely different. You probably won't find the spicy barbecue coleslaw (finely chopped cabbage slaw with a Lexington-style barbecue sauce added) at a chain cafeteria, for example. And the two large pieces of perfectly fried chicken that you can get at Bell's for around five dollars (including two vegetables) would cost a lot more than that anywhere else. A group of my companions joined me for lunch, and we played share the food. The beef stew received high marks as did the chicken and the vegetables. After a vote, we decided the barbecue slaw and the chopped cucumber-and-onion salad marinated in sweetened vinegar were exceptional. Nobody complained about the banana pudding and egg custard pie, either. Bell's has been a local favorite for nearly four decades. Little has changed, says Wayne Bell, who began working here with his father when he was in high school in 1980. "We've added some items over the years, and our dessert menu has grown. We're famous for our banana pudding and sweet potato pie." Other favorites are fried chicken and macaroni and cheese. "And we're the only place in town that serves

Wayne Bell with Flora Beathea at Bell & Sons Cafeteria

green peas and dumplings." The diverse clientele includes everyone from lawyers to laborers. If there's any secret to the cafeteria's longevity, Bell says it's "fresh food and family. We don't hire any managers or cooks. The family does all the cooking, and we don't spare anything costwise to make it good."

Southside Cafe
612 Waughtown Street
(336-788-9938)
Hours: Monday-Friday, 5:30 A.M.–2:30 P.M.

The same group that accompanied me to Bell & Sons Cafeteria also joined me for a late lunch at the Southside Cafe. Owners Wilma Hall and son Rusty Hall have operated the restaurant for more than three decades, and they have not wasted any money on fancy signs or landscaping. A crude wooden sign identifies the restaurant in a dirt parking lot speckled with weeds. An even cruder sign invites you to enter through a rear door. Inside, the restaurant is clean and bright with lots of paintings in which artist Mel Pittman appeared to have a surplus of blue. There's even a handsaw painted with a blue scene hanging over the door into the dining area.

The cafeteria line was not as extensive as the one at Bell & Sons. We

had a choice of one meat (veal cutlets, chicken, turkey and dressing,
or beef liver) and two vegetables
(greens, white beans, peas, and
fried potato pancakes). Everything
was good, but the tastiest items
were the potato pancakes and the
turkey and dressing.

Breakfast is the most popular
meal of the day, says Wilma Hall,
who figures she feeds an average
of 175 people a day. Locals especially like the fried fatback and the
scrambled brains and eggs. "We try
to fix everything from scratch," she
said. "I cook everything for my customers just like I would cook it for
myself."

Wilma and Rusty Hall, owners of
Southside Cafe

SOUTH CAROLINA

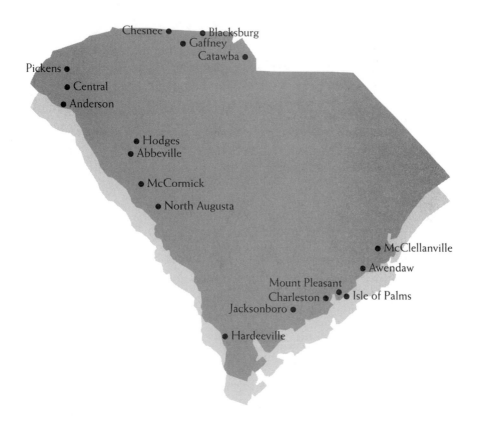

Chesnee ●   ● Blacksburg
● Gaffney
Catawba ●

Pickens ●

● Central
● Anderson

● Hodges
● Abbeville

● McCormick

● North Augusta

● McClellanville

● Awendaw

Mount Pleasant
Charleston ●   ● Isle of Palms
Jacksonboro ●

● Hardeeville

Abbeville

Buffet line at Yoder's Dutch Kitchen

Yoder's Dutch Kitchen

Highway 72
(864-459-5556)
Hours: Wednesday and Thursday, 11:00 A.M.–2:30 P.M.; Friday and Saturday,
  11:00 A.M.–2:30 P.M. and 5:00 P.M.–8:30 P.M.

Henry and Vera Yoder moved to Abbeville in 1969 and opened this restaurant that has become legendary for wonderful Mennonite food such as shoo-fly pie and apple fritters. The food is served cafeteria style, but instead of having a choice of only one meat entrée, you can get as many as you like. The only stipulation is that you don't take more than you can eat. If you go to Yoder's on the weekend, go early or be prepared to stand in line for an hour or so. Senior citizens love this place, and they also love to take their time choosing their selections. Every salad or dessert is minutely examined and discussed with their companions. Once you clear that hurdle, however, there's the food. Desserts first, tempting egg custard and shoo-fly pie and pecan pie and coconut cream and cobblers. The salad is next, and while it is mostly iceberg lettuce with a few cherry tomatoes and cucumbers, you have to get some just to have something to ladle the sweet-and-sour Dutch dressing on. I'd drink it out of the bottle if they'd let me, but it's probably best on the salad. After the salad, be prepared to make quick decisions. Do you want the eggplant casserole or the broccoli casserole? Corn or lima beans? Mashed potatoes or rice? Fried okra or macaroni and cheese? Chicken livers, fried chicken, meat loaf, fried fish, or turkey and dressing? Or a little of all? As you move your tray toward the bread, don't forget to get one or two of the apple fritters, tasty pastries rolled in powdered sugar. Now get your home-baked rolls and sweet tea and make yourself comfortable in one of the booths. And remember: you can always go back for

more, or ask one of the Mennonite waitresses to bring you another drumstick. All of this costs less than ten dollars, by the way, unless you decide to buy one of the whole pies, loaves of bread, apple fritters, or jars of homemade jellies and jams on your way out. Simply describing the food at Yoder's is not sufficient; you have to experience it yourself. And while you're in the area, take a tour of downtown Abbeville's old homes and antique shops and the restored Opera House.

Anderson

The Meeting Place
112 West Whitner Street
(864-226-3162)
Hours: Monday–Sunday, 7:30 A.M.–2:00 P.M.

The aptly named Meeting Place is a cafeteria located within walking distance of the courthouse and government offices in downtown Anderson. Fried chicken is always on the buffet line but, depending on which day you drop by, you might find chicken pot pie, country-style steak, salmon patties, meat loaf, or turkey and dressing. You can select three vegetables with your entrée, including macaroni and cheese, stewed corn, fresh vegetable soup, squash casserole, or sweet-potato soufflé. Top it off with a slice of chocolate pie, lemon pie, coconut pie, or a dish of peach cobbler.

Skin Thrasher's Hot Dogs
203 Hudgens Street
(864-225-9229)
Hours: Monday-Saturday, 11:00 A.M.–7:00 P.M.

What's a hot-dog place doing in a book about Southern food? Why, hot dogs are as much a part of Southern diets as collard greens and chicken. When I was growing up in McCormick County, South Carolina, getting a couple of greasy hot dogs was one of the biggest treats on a Saturday shopping trip to Greenwood or Anderson. The Greek hot-dog stand in Greenwood is not in business any more, but Skin Thrasher's is. Lloyd Thrasher, who acquired the nickname "Skin" after a barber cut his hair too short, has been serving hot dogs for more than fifty years. Of course, when he first opened in this mill village, it was a thriving community. He served sandwiches, too, but the hot dogs became so popular he made them his only menu item. So if you want a real Southern meal, stop by Skin's (don't let the decaying surroundings spook you) and order a couple of chili dogs and a Coke in a glass bottle. While you're inside, take a look at the pictures of all the celebrities who have eaten there.

Awendaw

Mary Rancourt, owner of See Wee Restaurant

See Wee Restaurant

4808 Highway 17 North
(803-928-3609)
Hours: Monday-Sunday, 11:30 A.M.–9:00 P.M.; breakfast served on Saturdays at
    7:00 A.M.

If you're in the Charleston area, it's worth your while to take a twenty-minute drive north on Highway 17 to the See Wee Restaurant. The little building looks like a country store, which it was for years. (The name *See Wee* came from an Indian tribe in the area.)

Owner Mary Rancourt has tried to maintain something of the nostalgic flavor of the old general store by keeping the shelves stocked with canned goods, baking powder, and old-fashioned grocery products. The day I stopped in, there were a half-dozen homemade cakes—pound and

caramel and chocolate pound and others—lined up on the counter. Meals include seafood as well as country cooking. You get a choice of four vegetables from a selection of fried squash, fried okra, red rice, butter beans,

sweet-potato casserole, fried green tomatoes, fried eggplant, collard greens, and more. Also available are shrimp or oyster baskets, soft-shell crab baskets, or a See Wee Platter with shrimp, oysters, scallops, and fish for around fifteen dollars. And for those with an aversion to fried foods, the See Wee serves a fresh fish of the day blackened, grilled, with Jamaican Jerk spice, or See Wee Style.

Blacksburg

Ed Brown's Restaurant and Western Store
Highway 5, downtown Blacksburg
(864-839-5646)
Hours: Monday-Friday, 8:00 A.M.–4:00 P.M.; Saturday, 8:00 A.M–2:00 P.M.

To get to Blacksburg, take the Highway 5 exit off Interstate 85 north of Gaffney and drive until your eyes cross. I wouldn't recommend a special trip, but if you're on your way to Rock Hill or Charlotte and want to see some of the countryside, this isn't a bad route. And Ed Brown's isn't a bad restaurant. Where else can you buy a pair of Tony Lama boots or a ten-gallon hat and get some delicious salmon stew, too? Ed's actually is more of a short-order lunch and breakfast counter tucked over in the corner of his western-wear store. He has homemade soups every day, salmon stew and chicken stew two or three times a week, and Beanee Weenees all the time. You can get a homemade pimento-cheese sandwich to go with the soup, or, if you're real hungry, get a Spam burger or bologna burger with lettuce and tomato. For breakfast, Ed serves biscuits and ham and bacon and eggs, of course, but you can also try a livermush sandwich.

Catawba

Fast Buck's
5595 Highway 5
(803-366-4405)
Hours: Monday-Friday, 5:00 A.M.–1:00 A.M.; Saturday and Sunday, 7:00 A.M.–
  midnight.

Fast Buck's looks like a truck stop, which it is, but it's also a restaurant and hunting-supply store. Friends at the South Carolina Tourism Department had recommended Fast Buck's, so I cheerfully drove through a Carolina monsoon to find the place, only to discover that there was a Blimpie's inside. I was about to walk out when I noticed a gray-haired lady, serving up fried chicken and vegetables. Yes, she told me, she had cooked everything, and it was too bad I had not gotten here earlier. Between the hunters and the truck drivers, just about everything was gone. Any other time I could have gotten meat loaf, country steak, salisbury steak, or stew beef. There was enough left for me, however, and I got some chicken and mashed potatoes and greens and iced tea on a tray and was directed to the dining area upstairs where I sat at a wooden table overlooked by a mounted deer head, a stuffed fox, turkey targets, and enough camouflage equipment to outfit a small militia. Although the food was quite tasty, it's a little unnerving to eat while Bambi's mother is watching you with those big brown eyes.

Central

Chris and Doug Rybolt with their daughter Sophia

Central Station Cafe
West Main Street
(864-639-6780)
Hours: Monday and Tuesday, 11:00 A.M.–2:00 P.M.; Wednesday-Friday, 11:00 A.M.–
9:00 P.M.; Sunday, 11:00 A.M.–2:00 P.M.; closed Saturdays.

Located three miles from Clemson, the Central Station Cafe is worth a side trip. Just don't go on a Saturday when the Tigers are playing, because the restaurant is closed. The food is served cafeteria style and includes the usual assortments of fried chicken and vegetables. The difference is in the small touches that owners Doug and Chris Rybolt have added over the last seven years. For example, Doug, a former executive chef for several Hilton hotels, put fried bologna on the menu just as an experiment a couple of years ago, and the customers went crazy for it. Other special dishes include sausage gravy with country-style steak, smoked sausage and sauerkraut, and grilled flounder.

Charleston

Julian Atlow, Brenda Howle, Juliana Atlow, and Paul Howle
enjoy roasted oysters at Bowen's Island Restaurant.

Bowen's Island Restaurant

1870 Bowen's Island Road
(803-795-2757)
Hours: Monday-Saturday, 5:00 P.M.–10:00 P.M.

Bowen's Island has been a Charleston institution since 1946 when it was founded by May and Jimmy Bowen. Their grandson, Robert Barber, runs the place now, and from the looks of things, nothing has been changed since 1946—not even the Seeberg jukebox which still plays five 78's (*Mr. Sandman* is on there) for a quarter. Generations of customers over the years have left their names and bits of graffiti on the discolored walls.

Located on a bumpy dirt road at the tip of a thirteen-acre island, the restaurant has a great view of the river, marshes, and islands. But the view is not why so many people come here. They come here for the roasted oysters—huge shovelfuls of roasted oysters dumped on rickety tables covered with newspaper and served

The Coke machine, jukebox, and graffiti-covered walls at Bowen's Island Restaurant

with saltines and hot sauce. For fifteen dollars, you can eat all you want; you just have to shuck them yourself and dump the shells in a five-gallon bucket. For those who aren't oyster lovers, and I really feel sorry for them, there are other seafood items available in the adjoining dining area. Fried seafood platters, steamed blue crabs, crab cakes, and shrimp and grits come highly recommended by Charlestonians.

Chesnee

Bantam Chef
Four blocks off of Scenic Highway 11 on U.S. 221
(864-461-8403)
Hours: Monday-Sunday, 6:00 A.M.–10:30 P.M.

Drowsy travelers stopping to eat breakfast at the Bantam Chef might think they have stepped into a time warp. An old Mobil gas station adjoins the restaurant, which is decorated as a 1950s diner. Inside you'll find a perfectly restored 1950 Studebaker, complete with an Elvis dummy behind the wheel, a 1958 BMW, a Wurlitzer jukebox with '50s hits, and other memorabilia. If you want to see other Studebakers, just ask owner David Walker: he has more than sixty of the restored classics. In keeping with the nostalgia of the '50s, Walker sells coffee for twenty-five cents and serves hand-shaped hamburgers and cheeseburgers, malts and banana splits like you remember eating after the big game in high school. For breakfast, try the cathead biscuits (this refers to the size, not the ingredients), sausage and gravy, eggs, or pancakes. Local favorites are the livermush and the fried bologna. Lunch specials vary, but usually include fried chicken, country-fried steak, chicken and dumplings, or stew beef, and an assortment of vegetables. By the way, if you have some munchkins in tow, they can get a kid's cruiser meal served in a toy '57 Chevy.

Turner Family Restaurant
221 Alabama Avenue
(864-461-8815)
Hours: Monday-Saturday, 5:30 A.M.–9:00 P.M.; Sunday, 11:00 A.M.–2:00 P.M.

It's unusual for a small town to have two good down-home restaurants, but Chesnee does. Right across the street from the Bantam Chef is Turner's Family Restaurant, another favorite of the lunch crowd. There are no restored classic Studebakers here, but you can get a meat-and-three meal that includes one of the daily specials—fried chicken, stew beef, chicken livers, meat loaf, salmon patties, and more—and a choice of vegetables. The pear salad, deviled eggs, squash casserole, and okra are highly recommended. Not in the mood for big meal? Turner's serves vegetable soup and cornbread every day.

Gaffney

Starlite Diner
Exit 90 off Interstate 85; diner is behind the Carolina Factory Outlet
(864-489-7585)
Hours: Monday-Sunday, 7:00 A.M.–9:00 P.M.

You take your chances when you stop at a restaurant at one of the interstate exits, but the Starlite Diner is a notch above the usual tourist places. Bright and shiny with black-and-white checkerboard floor tiles and the requisite jukebox, the diner offers burgers and fries and short orders with catchy musical names, such as the Beach Boy Basket and Blueberry Hill Pancakes. You can't go wrong with the burgers, which are thick and juicy, and during lunch you might try one of the Platters with a choice of pork chops, country-fried steak, meat loaf, or hamburger steak, and two vegetables. And while you're waiting for your order and listening to Little Anthony and the Imperials, check out the signs around the counter: "If the music's too loud, you're too old," and "The quickest way to get on your feet is to miss two car payments."

Hardeeville

Other Voices, Other Tastes

The Cripple Crab

By Michael Johnson

The Cripple Crab is located on Highway 17 North. (803-784-2708)

The Cripple Crab in Hardeeville is a fun place to eat. It's decorated with movie posters, and there happens to be a picture of Mr. Clark Gable there. They have great iced tea. I had fried chicken, corn, and lima beans. I believe it was the best chicken I found in South Carolina. My guest had pork chops with gravy that were superb. Nice-sized portions, too. If Mr. Rhett Butler were alive today, he would be there several times a week. Forget Scarlett. The food there is better than anything he could get at Tara.

Michael Johnson of Atlanta makes frequent personal appearances as Rhett Butler.

Hodges

Somebody's House

5200 Emerson Street
(864-374-7434)
Hours: Tuesday-Friday, 11:30 A.M.–1:00 P.M.; Sunday, 11:00 A.M. –2:30 P.M.

Somebody's House really does look like somebody's house. It's a simple frame dwelling in this little town north of Greenwood. If you're in the area for the Festival of Flowers in July or are visiting the famous Park Seed Company, it's worth the ten-minute drive to eat lunch or Sunday dinner at Louise Youngblood's. A buffet of two or three meats and a half-dozen vegetables and salads is set up in the dining room. Find a table in one of the other rooms, place your drink order, and then take your plate and fill it with fried chicken, baked chicken, macaroni and cheese, sweet-potato soufflé, broccoli casserole, lima beans, or greens, and homemade biscuits or cornbread. It's good country food, fresh and well-seasoned. If you can resist eating more than one piece of fried chicken, you have more will power than I do.

After stuffing myself, I caught up with Mrs. Youngblood in the kitchen and asked her if she had time to answer a few questions. An hour later, she paused long enough for me to get a word in. It seems that more than a quarter century ago, she decided to go into the restaurant and catering business. By careful planning, buying stoves and furniture at yard sales, and picking up silver and china that was dented or chipped, she launched a

Louise Youngblood, owner of Somebody's House

successful business. (The place is so packed on a Sunday, that many of the customers simply mill around in the front yard looking at the flowers until a table is cleared). "I still shop carefully," says Mrs. Youngblood, who is in her late seventies. "Whatever meat special I can buy at the grocery store, that's what I'll have the next week. It could be chicken or pork chops or something else. And I try to get the freshest vegetables I can. The worst thing you can do is serve something you wouldn't serve your own family."

Isle of Palms

The Sea Biscuit Cafe

21 J.C. Long Boulevard
(803-886-4079)
Hours: Tuesday-Friday, 6:30 A.M.–2:00 P.M.; Saturday and Sunday, 7:30 A.M.–
1:00 P.M.

Just across the bridge from Mount Pleasant, a suburb of Charleston, The Isle of Palms and Sullivan's Island are rich in history and, well, just plain rich. This is where wealthy Charlestonians spend their summers and where many of them rent their houses to tourists in the off-season. At the tip of Sullivan's Island is Fort Moultrie, established by the British in colonial days. Edgar Allan Poe wrote *The Gold Bug* on Sullivan's Island while stationed at Fort Moultrie, and slaves who were being brought to America were quarantined on the island before being auctioned in Charleston.

Another landmark is the Sea Biscuit Cafe. There's nothing historic about it, but after you eat breakfast here, you'll remember it long after your tour of Fort Moultrie. Located in a tiny cottage a block or so from the beach, the Sea Biscuit serves homemade corned-beef hash, thick-sliced bacon, eggs benedict, and biscuits that are truly memorable. Daily specials and various kinds of omelettes are also available.

Jacksonboro

Edisto Motel Restaurant

S.C. Highway 17, about thirty miles south of Charleston
(803-893-2270)
Hours: Thursday–Saturday, 5:00 P.M.–9:00 P.M.

Other Voices Other Tastes

By Hoppin' John Martin Taylor

I don't go out to eat much since I cook. But I do like to go to the Edisto Motel Restaurant to get fried fish. Everything's fried. They have fish, oysters, shad roe, catfish, and shrimp. Oh, and I ate at the See Wee Cafe once, and it was excellent.

Hoppin' John Martin Taylor is the author of *The Fearless Frying Cookbook*. He lives in Charleston.

Other Voices Other Tastes

By Wendell Brock

After fifty-one years on the scene, Zelma Hickman and family really have mastered the art of frying. No wonder Charleston cookbook writer Hoppin' John Martin Taylor dedicated his book, *The Fearless Frying Cookbook*, to the women of the Edisto, where the menu says: "No broiled foods."

At seventy-one, Hickman still waits tables with unfailing politeness, tenderly ministering to small and adult-size children. She inherited the restaurant from her parents, her sister got the motel, and her brother got the filling station (after it fell into disrepair, he just set fire to it, Hickman says).

The Edisto Motel Restaurant is open but three nights a week, so you can count on sitting a spell out front, even if you arrive before the doors are unlocked at 5:00 P.M. There's no waiting list, which makes everybody kind of ornery with anticipation.

So pop a soda or a beer from the fridge inside the waiting room (just tell them how many you drank before you leave). When you no longer recognize anybody else in line, it must be your turn. With knotty-pine walls and green-vinyl booths, it's an old-fashioned fish camp, where you're liable to see families of ten at a table, the kids noshing on burgers and fries, and the grown-ups inhaling the fried fish.

Order the fried seafood platter and you'll get a veritable trough of oysters, scallops, a chunk of flounder, a fluffy deviled crab, and piles of shrimp, smaller than the norm but quite delicious. You will not need a first course but, if you must, the long-simmered tomato-based catfish stew is a cup of comfort. Don't hesitate to crumble up the hush puppies on top, as you would saltines.

Wendell Brock is a reporter for the *Atlanta Journal-Constitution*.

McClellanville

Buster's Porchside Dining
Main Street in McClellanville
(803-887-3331)
Hours: Monday-Friday, 7:30 A.M.–2:00 P.M.; Thursday, 5:00 P.M.–9:00 P.M.; Friday and
Saturday, 6:00 P.M.–9:00 P.M.; Sunday, 11:00 A.M.–1:00 P.M. The restaurant is
closed on Thanksgiving, Christmas, New Year's Day, and July 4.

McClellanville is a quaint little coastal town about forty miles north of Charleston on Highway 17. It was almost blown away by Hugo, but the residents—shrimpers, merchants, retirees, and a few artists and writers such as William Baldwin (*The Hard to Catch Mercy*) and Theodore Rosengarten (*Tombee*)—didn't let a hurricane dampen their spirits. Several store owners were out sweeping the sidewalks and speaking to an occasional wandering dog (McClellanville has no leash law) when my friends and I arrived. I unexpectedly ran into author Billy Baldwin at a

*Author William Baldwin rests after a meal at
Buster's Porchside Dining.*

local real-estate office and invited him to lunch. When he suggested Buster's, my friends were a little hesitant. After all, one does not expect to encounter a memorable meal in the back of a grocery store.

But we were pleasantly surprised. Located in the rear (actually, off to the side) of T.W. Graham and Co. Grocery, the restaurant was opened in 1994 by Buster Browne and his wife Sherry. "We started out serving burgers and sandwiches and it kind of blossomed into what we are now," Browne says.

What they are now is a restaurant that serves the freshest seafood for miles around. Diners are seated at long wooden tables in a large, L-shaped screened room. One of the chefs, Pete Kornack, is a graduate of the Calfornia Culinary Institute, and the other, Grace Smith, is a Colombia, South America, native who has added an exotic Latin flavor to much of the food. She is responsible for the jalapeño-cheese biscuits and the shrimp quesadillas.

"All of the recipes are ours," Browne says, "and we get all of our seafood fresh. We're known for our she-crab soup and our crab cakes. We don't use any bread in our crab cakes. We only use egg for binder. That's one thing Sherry and I agreed on, we got tired of eating crab cakes with very little crabmeat in them."

Anything on the menu is good, but the lightly battered fried shrimp, fried oysters, and fried soft-shell crab are especially delicious. A nice touch is the fresh fruit garnish of kiwi, cantaloupe, and orange slices. On the weekends, Buster's offers crab-stuffed flounder or crab cakes with black beans and rice and grilled veggies. And be sure to save enough room for the Key lime pie or coconut custard pie for dessert.

McCormick

Edmunds and Callie's on Main
222 Main Street
(864-465-3225)
Hours: Monday-Friday, 7:00 A.M.–2:00 P.M.; Saturday, 7:00 A.M.–2:00 P.M. and
   5:00 P.M.–10:00 P.M.

McCormick was a gold-mining town in the 1800s, and there are still shafts and tunnels under some of the streets. Every summer the town celebrates its heritage with Gold Rush Days, a festival of crafts and food and music. Situated less than ten miles from the Savannah River and Lake Thurmond (the locals still call it Clark Hill Reservoir), the town is a sportsman's paradise. The woods are bountiful with deer and wild turkeys, and the lakes are teeming with fish. Lately, with the development of a retirement/resort community on the lake, and Hickory Knob State Park, the area has become something of a golfer's paradise, too. There are even some fancy restaurants within an hour's drive, but most of the locals go to Edmunds and Callie's for breakfast or for the meat-and-three lunches of baked ham, fried chicken livers, fried chicken, rice and gravy, macaroni and cheese, black-eyed peas, string beans, broccoli casserole, sweet-potato soufflé, and chocolate cake. Saturday nights are special. That's when you can get all-you-can-eat seafood for about twelve dollars. Maybe it's not as fancy as some of the more elegant restaurants just across the river in Augusta, but it's homemade and filling. No, there's not much to do in McCormick after dark, but you can always drive over to the lake, tune in the oldies station, find a parking place, and watch the moon drift across the sky with someone you love. Now that's what I call after-dinner entertainment.

Mount Pleasant

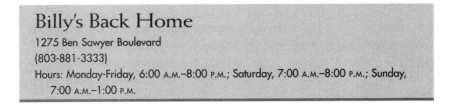

Billy's Back Home
1275 Ben Sawyer Boulevard
(803-881-3333)
Hours: Monday-Friday, 6:00 A.M.–8:00 P.M.; Saturday, 7:00 A.M.–8:00 P.M.; Sunday, 7:00 A.M.–1:00 P.M.

Martha Stewart would go crazy in Billy's. Not because of the food, which is quite tasty, but because of the decor. I guess you could describe it as eclectic. Old car tags from Puerto Rico to New Hampshire line one wall. There are framed ads for a 1939 Dodge on another, along with a mounted striped bass and a shotgun, and a sled and snow skis are suspended from the ceiling.

But if you aren't Martha Stewart, and maybe even if you are, you won't be disappointed in the breakfasts here. When you order a sausage and biscuit, you get *two* sausage patties on a cathead biscuit. The Homecakes and HomeSpun French Toast are house specialties, but my favorite breakfast was the scrambled eggs, grits, bacon, sausage gravy, and biscuits. Not something Martha would order, I'm sure.

Billy's also has changing daily lunch and dinner specials that include fried pork chops, roast pork, meat loaf, country-fried steak, and hamburger steak with grilled onions and gravy. You get a choice of three side dishes such as squash casserole, macaroni and cheese, steamed cabbage, field peas, candied yams, or fried okra.

North Augusta

Old McDonald Fish Camp

355 Currytown Road
(803-279-3305)
Hours: Thursday-Saturday, 5:30 P.M.–10:00 P.M.

The original Old McDonald in the nursery rhyme had a farm. Well, so does Jerry Bass, the owner of this sprawling fish camp in Edgefield County. His collection of animals include a pot-bellied pig, Texas longhorns, goats, peacocks, ducks, chickens, and geese. Although the restaurant seats about two hundred fifty, sometimes there's a wait and the kids—and grownups—can pass the time feeding and watching the animals. Or you stand on a covered bridge over a moat that Bass dug to connect to a large pond and watch for fish.

Inside, it's easier to spot the fish. Fried catfish is the most popular item, served with grits and hush puppies. But you can also order broiled or fried shrimp or fish, frog legs, and scallops.

Pickens

Table Rock Lodge Restaurant

Route 3, sixteen miles north of Pickens on S.C. 11

(803-878-9065)

Hours (November 1-April 30): Tuesday-Saturday, 4:00 P.M.–9:00 P.M.; Sunday buffet, 11:30 A.M.–3:00 P.M.; Sunday dinner, 5:00 P.M.–9:00 P.M. Hours (May 1-October 31): Tuesday-Sunday, 11:30 A.M.–9:00 P.M.; closed Mondays.

Located in Table Rock State Park, this stone-and-timber lodge has breathtaking views of the mountains and a small lake. The rock itself was once a part of the Cherokee Indian land before the Europeans came to South Carolina, and was an easily visible landmark, which the Indians used to find their way. According to legend, the Great Spirit used Table Rock's flat mountaintop for dining. The Table Rock Lodge Restaurant offers a number of seafood items including fried shrimp, oysters, and mountain trout. But as any frequent traveler knows, usually it's best to order food that is available locally. Sometimes you can get good seafood miles from the coast, and sometimes you can't. So if you're not willing to gamble, I recommend the trout that is shipped in from just over the state line in North Carolina. The one I had was so big it hung over the edge of the plate and tasted as fresh as if it had just been pulled out of the lake down below. Other selections on the lunch menu include hamburger steak or daily specials of a meat and three home-cooked vegetables.

TENNESSEE

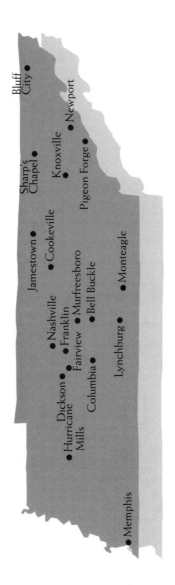

Chris Wohlwend, a freelance food writer for *The Atlanta Journal-Constitution* and other publications, contributed his expertise on Sea Boat Steak House, Ruby's Cafe, Southern Vittles Restaurant, Litton's, Leach Family Restaurant, Tucker's Main Street Cafe, and Cole's Store.

Bell Buckle

Bell Buckle Cafe
Downtown Bell Buckle
(615-389-9693)
Hours: Monday, 8:00 A.M.–5:00 P.M.; Tuesday-Thursday, 8:00 A.M.–8:00 P.M.; Sunday, 11:00 A.M.–5:00 P.M.

Bell Buckle is a charming little town in the rolling green hills south of Nashville near Shelbyville, the Tennessee Walking Horse capital of the world. The third Saturday in June every year more than eighty thousand visitors come for the Moon Pie Festival here. (For non-Southerners who may not be familiar with Moon Pies, they are a chocolate-covered graham-cracker sandwiches with marshmallow filling. It's about the size of the palm of your hand, and it goes down wonderfully with an RC Cola.) The rest of the time, tourists come to browse through the antique shops and bookstore or to visit students at The Webb School.

Or they come to eat at the Bell Buckle Cafe and listen to bluegrass music.

J. Gregory Heinike, his wife Jeanette, and daughters Heidi and Heather bought the cafe in 1993 and quickly made it a gathering place for the county and surrounding areas. Daily specials, posted on a blackboard outside the screen door leading into the cafe, include things like catfish or pork chops, red beans and rice, or other country vegetables. The smoked chop—a grilled pork chop lightly smoked over the grill—is one of the best I've had. The barbecue, cooked slowly on an outside grill, comes with sliced onions, pickles, and vinegar slaw. The homemade lemonade, served in Mason jars with handles, is tangy and delicious. But of all the items on the menu, if you have to have just one, try the oatmeal cake with caramel sauce. You'll lick the saucer it's so good.

The Heinikes have decorated the cafe with antique items, posters, autographed pictures of country-music stars, and old bird houses. Gregory acts as deejay for a live radio show on WLIJ (1580 AM) from the cafe every Saturday from 1:00 P.M. to 3:00 P.M.; Thursday night is singer/ songwriters night; and there's live music from various singers and groups on Friday, Saturday, and Sunday. The Heinikes have even started their own record label, Bell Buckle Records, and sell CDs at the counter. While you're there, pick up some of the Heinike's special spices—Country Magic for chops or Country Jazz for red beans and rice. And don't let the screen door slam on your way out.

Bluff City

Ridgewood Barbecue
900 Elizabethton Highway
(423-538-7543)
Hours: Tuesday-Thursday, 11:30 A.M.–7:30 P.M.; Friday and Saturday, 11:30 A.M.–
2:30 P.M. and 4:30 P.M.–8:30 P.M.

Ridgewood Barbecue owner Grace Profitt has been interviewed by everyone from Joan Lunden to ESPN analyst Benny Parsons. *People* maga-zine proclaimed Ridgewood as having the best barbecue in the country. Not many people will disagree. Mrs. Proffitt serves a Texas-style sweet-and-sour barbecue with a sauce she created by trial and error. She has kept the recipe secret from everyone except her son Terry. Former Ten-nessee governor Lamar Alexander has praised her barbecue as has Sissy Spacek, who ate there while she was filming *The River*. The Proffitts opened the restaurant in 1948 when the area was so poor the women who worked as her waitresses didn't have transportation. Mrs. Proffitt simply woke up early every morning and picked them up in her car.

It would be a shame to go to Ridgewood and not order the barbecue, but there are other items on the menu that are good, too. If you really aren't in the mood for barbecue, try the pork-chop platter, the shrimp platter, the fried-oyster platter, or the catfish dinner. Whatever you or-der, you must try the beans. They are simmered slowly in a thick sauce with bits of onions and served in individual crocks. If you go on weekends, go early. Sometimes there's a line. After you eat there, you'll know why.

Columbia

Buckey's Restaurant
1102 Carmack Boulevard
(931-381-2834)
Hours: Monday-Saturday, 5:00 A.M.–8:00 P.M.

Whether the specialty of the house is good Southern cooking or local politics is sometimes confused. But even Republicans and Democrats agree that the meat-and-three lunch specials at Buckey's can't be beat. One of the favorite specials is roast beef and gravy—and this is beef that is roasted on the premises—with a choice of vegetables from a selection of as many as a dozen. Also recommended is the chicken and dressing. Top it off with one of the homemade pies or a bowl of peach cobbler or banana pudding. No wonder the big red rooster on the sign has been crowing about Rick and Janice Cunningham's restaurant for more than twenty-five years.

Cookeville

City Square Cafe
453 East Broad Street
(615-528-9120)
Hours: Monday-Friday, 5:00 A.M.–2:00 P.M.; Sunday, 5:00 A.M.–1:00 P.M.

Roger Holloway, his wife Sue, and daughter Jennifer Holloway opened this downtown restaurant in 1993 after years of cooking and serving food at a booth at the county fair. Breakfast here is the meal of the day, with crusty tender biscuits and all of the accompaniments. Lunch is buffet style, with pot roast, chicken and dumplings, goulash, meat loaf, and fried chicken. And you have a choice of the standard Southern vegetables, plus hominy, macaroni and tomatoes, and mixed beans. The food is not exceptional but it's not bad—and it's filling. The service is friendly and efficient despite a sign at the cash register that says, "I can only please one person a day, and today ain't your day."

Dickson

The double fireplace in East Hills' large dining room

East Hills Restaurant
Intersection of Highway 70 and Highway 46
(615-441-9428)
Hours: Monday-Thursday, 6:00 A.M.–8:30 P.M.; Friday and Saturday, 6:00 P.M.–
   9:00 P.M.; Sunday, 11:00 A.M.–8:30 P.M.

John and Anita Luther's restaurant is one of those family-owned eating establishments where the vegetables are fresh and the waitresses are friendly. Open since the 1940s, East Hills Restaurant has a large dining room with a double fireplace, a meeting room lined with pictures of civic leaders, and a sideboard room filled with, well, antique sideboards. The weekend buffet draws the biggest crowds with a lineup of fried fish, barbecued chicken, carved roast beef, pulled pork barbecue, marinated pork chops, and a soup-and-salad bar. The rest of the week you can have daily specials such as salmon croquettes, chicken and dumplings, turkey and dressing, sugar-cured ham, or calf's liver with onions. If you're eating light, as I was the day I visited, you can't go wrong with the homemade vegetable soup, hot cornbread sticks, and

a homemade chicken-salad sandwich with a pear half and cottage cheese. Of course, all that light eating was cancelled out with the large slice of coconut cream pie I had. Quite tasty, with meringue as light as angel wings.

Fairview

Country Cafe

794 Fairview Boulevard East

(615-799-0215)

Hours: Daily from 7:00 A.M.–8:00 P.M.

You almost are compelled to stop at a restaurant called the Country Cafe across from an antique store called Mama-n-Nems. Open since 1997,

Gary Tidwell, owner of the Country Cafe

the Country Cafe has quickly attracted a loyal following, thanks to the culinary experience of owner Grady Tidwell. Tidwell operated several chain restaurants around Tennessee before deciding to move back to his hometown to open his own. He leaves the cooking to his wife, Virginia Tidwell, a native of Louisiana who uses family recipes and refuses to cut corners. "We pan fry our chicken," Tidwell says. "A lot of people say you can't tell the difference between pan-fried and deep-fried, but you can." He's right, you know. Tidwell's chicken is just like Mama used to fry. So far, Tidwell says, his biggest nights are Fridays, when he serves hand-breaded catfish, oysters, and shrimp, and Saturdays, when he cooks prime rib.

"There really isn't any secret to running a good restaurant," Tidwell says. "You just need good food and consistency. Nobody wants to try the same dish twice and find out you've changed the recipe. They want food that tastes the same week in and week out."

Franklin

The staff at Dotson's

Dotson's
99 East Main Street
(615-794-2805)
Hours: Monday-Friday, 6:00 A.M.–8:30 P.M.; Saturday, 6:00 A.M.–3:00 P.M.; Sunday,
7:00 A.M.–3:00 P.M

Dotson's country cooking attracts regular customers for breakfast, lunch, and dinner. Some of the folks eat all three meals there. The day I dropped in, there was a pork-chop-and-gravy special as well as a choice of fried chicken, meat loaf, barbecue chicken, chicken and dumplings, spaghetti, gizzards and gravy, and wieners and kraut. Vegetable selections included spinach, turnip greens, apples, green beans, cabbage, mashed potatoes, corn on the cob, lima beans, white beans, black-eyed peas, cream corn, sweet-potato casserole, squash, beets, and more.

Dotson's is also famous for its fried pies—apple, cherry, and peach—as well as their chocolate and lemon pies. The chocolate pie was heavenly and the fried peach pie I got to go was very tasty even a couple of hours later.

Dotson's has been a landmark in Franklin for more than forty years. One of the reasons is the food, of course. At least twenty different vegetable or salad selections are offered every day with lunch specials that include at least six different kinds of meats. But perhaps a big reason for the success is current owner Arthur McCloud, who rescued the restaurant from bankruptcy a couple of decades ago and put it back on solid financial footing. It didn't hurt that McCloud was in the restaurant-equipment business and had seen the workings of hundreds of eating establishments when the bankruptcy court asked him to take over. "Nearly every successful restaurant operation I saw was a mom-and-pop operation where the owners were always on the premises. The ones that left things in the hands of hired help didn't do as well."

Hurricane Mills

The Log Cabin Restaurant
Interstate 40 and Highway 13
(931-296-5311)
Hours: Daily from 6:00 A.M.–9:00 P.M.

By Miriam Longino

If you're on the long drive from Nashville to Memphis and want a departure from cardboard-flavored food, check out this haven of home-cooking. Located about one hour west of Nashville, the restaurant sits right off the interstate in a neon-and-concrete jungle of gas stations and motels. But you'll spot it right away because the restaurant is housed in an actual one-hundred-year-old hickory log cabin. You're not going to find the word "lite" on this menu. Specialties are meat-and-vegetable plates like your mother would serve the preacher for Sunday dinner. Here's a clue as to how seriously the kitchen takes its work: if you order fried chicken, the friendly waitress will jump in immediately to tell you it requires a twenty-minute wait in order to be cooked. The country-fried steak is a gravy-lover's dream—a hand-pounded-and-breaded beef cutlet smothered in light-brown milk gravy. Also, remember you're in the heart of catfish country here, and the piping hot and tender fried filets are served up with fries, coleslaw, and just-right hush puppies. Another Tennessee treat: the country-ham plate with red-eye gravy. Each main dish comes with a choice of two vegetables, from made-from-scratch mashed potatoes to turnip greens to white beans seasoned with flecks of ham and onion. There are thick burgers for the kids, and the coffee is always brewing. Other entrées are catfish, country-fried steak, and fried chicken. Hurricane Mills is the home of the Loretta Lynn Dude Ranch. Avoid the Loretta Lynn's Kitchen restaurant at all costs.

—*Miriam Longino is a reporter for the* Atlanta Journal-Constitution.

Jamestown

Sea Boat Steak House
Highway 127 South
(931-879-3640)
Hours: Daily, 10:00 A.M.–10:00 P.M.

Jamestown is high on the Cumberland Plateau, hours of tricky roads from just about anywhere. The nearest ocean is seven hundred or so miles away. So how can there be a seafood restaurant? When I asked, Christy just said, "because we know how to fix the best food around here." And she was right. Catfish and hush puppies and homemade corn relish and a sweet and vinegary slaw were excellent. A trip to the lunchtime buffet yielded superb meat loaf and mashed potatoes. So check out the collection of ship models, ignore the fact that you're far removed from the ocean, and enjoy the food.

The menu includes everything from Calabash shrimp to alligator and shark. Catfish is served with fries, slaw, and hush puppies. The Sea Boat platter is piled high with shrimp, fish, clams, scallops, oysters, crab, fries, slaw, and hush puppies.

Knoxville

Photo by Ben Wohlwend
The ladies who run Ruby's Cafe

Ruby's Cafe

3920 Martin Luther King Avenue
(423-522-0782)
Hours: Monday-Friday, 6:00 A.M.–2:00 p.m.; Saturday, 6:00 a.m.–11:00 a.m.

Ruby's is the kind of place where the firemen from down the street are often found behind the counter helping themselves to coffee. It's all family. Ruby Henderlight opened the cafe in 1961 after running a grocery store. She's moved once (across the street) and over the years added different family members to the staff. The crowds have remained constant, and though she's mostly retired today, her sister, daughters, and granddaughters are carrying on the family tradition.

Luncheon rib-stickers include meat loaf, country-fried steak, chicken (fried, baked with dressing, or stewed with dumplings) and fried cornbread. Ruby's daughter Mary Jo Netherton bakes the fruit cobblers and other desserts. Mary Jo's younger sister, Barbara Williams and her aunt, Ann Henderlight, do most of the other cooking.

On Saturdays (breakfast only), Mary Jo's daughter, Vicki Lawson, runs the grill and, if she likes you, can sometimes be cajoled into fixing a cheeseburger, even if it's 8:30 in the morning. Vicki started helping out at the age of nine, standing on boxes so she could reach the sink to wash the pots.

Southern Vittles Restaurant

3701-B Chapman Highway
(423-579-9005)
Hours: Monday-Friday, 7:00 A.M.–8:00 P.M.; Sunday brunch, noon–2:00 P.M.

Kathy and Ben Burks have been open only a couple of years, but they drew crowds almost from Day One with honest home-style cooking: meat loaf, country-style steak, chicken and dumplings, hand-mashed potatoes, turnip greens, and banana pudding. The slaw, a red cabbage, sweet-and-sour concoction, is a righteous addition to any meal. The phone number listed is a recording of the weekly menu, so if there's something you don't like, you can skip that day. Chances are, though, you won't hear anything you don't like.

Photo by Chris Wohlwend
The sign in front of Litton's proclaims the "10"
burger in no uncertain terms.

Litton's

2803 Essary Drive
(423-688-0429)
Hours: Monday-Saturday, 11:00 A.M.–9:00 P.M.

The sign out front proclaims the "10" burger in no uncertain terms, telling one and all which side of the bun Litton's is on. The burgers, made with top-quality meat and cooked to order, are offered in the standard variety. You can add cheese, bacon, etc. For fans of Robert Mitchum, there's the Thunder Road, which comes equipped with pimento cheese, grilled onions, and jalapeno peppers. Named after the 1959 Mitchum moonshiner movie set in east Tennessee, it's more of a load than a trunkful of white lightnin'.

Famous though Litton's hamburgers are, this decades-old joint is equally known for desserts. When she finishes up the day's supply of hamburger buns, baker Mary Jones turns her attention to sweets. Her traditional Southern cakes—chocolate, red velvet, carrot—are high and mighty. She also makes cheesecakes, pies, and cookies, all rivals to the best anywhere.

Lunchtime specials sometimes offer Arizona spuds as a vegetable option. If it's on the board, don't miss this cheese-rich casserole. A straight-up burger is $5.29, and the Thunder Road with a side is about $8.00. It's worth it.

Lynchburg

Other Voices, Other Tastes

Mary Bobo's

By John Egerton

One of my favorite places is Mary Bobo's in Lynchburg. The place really does feel like a country home. The town, famous for the nearby Jack Daniels distillery, is rather idyllic. It's built around the court-house square. Off on one of those streets is Miss Mary's, which sits under some maple trees. It's a white frame house with a garden off to one side. When you go there in the summer it's delightful because when the garden is in its prime, you're eating the freshest food you can get. Freshness is everything. When you eat green beans there, you know they haven't been processed through a farmers' market. They have a different flavor. Miss Mary Bobo held forth there until she was well past one hundred, then she died and a young woman named Lynne Tolley reopened it and re-hired Miss Mary's cooks. The fried chicken there is great. They cook it in lard, I think, the old-fashioned way in black iron skillets.

John Egerton is the author of *Southern Food,* among other works. He lives in Nashville.

Memphis

Ellen's Soul Food Restaurant
601 South Parkway East
(901-942-4888)
Hours: Monday-Thursday, 6:00 A.M.–9:00 P.M.; Friday and Saturday, 6:00 A.M.–
    midnight; Sunday, 6:00 A.M.–6:00 P.M.

By Frederic Koeppel

Sometimes there's nothing like a good meat loaf to make you feel that all's right with the world. If you agree, you might want to drop in at Ellen's Soul Food Restaurant—affectionately called Miss Ellen's—for a slab of the hearty, thickly grained oniony stuff, liberally sprinkled with black pepper.

Miss Ellen's qualifies as a clean, well-lighted place. Shaker-plain except for groups of posters, mottos, and pictures on the wall behind the counter. Booths are painted bright colors, rhythm-and-blues churn from the radio and, one day when I was there, an old man sat in a dark cubbyhole, picking through greens like a figure symbolizing human endurance in a Faulkner novel.

Be certain to accompany your meat loaf or whatever you order with the gratis plateful of piping hot cornmeal pancakes straight from the kitchen. These are not sweet: they are dense but finely textured, nutty and toothsome, and downright addictive.

Fried chicken must be pronounced not the best in town but close enough not to matter except to the most finicky. The skin is crisp and refreshingly free of grease, the succulent flesh almost as tender and moist as one could want.

The barbecue at Miss Ellen's is curious but good. The sauce possesses a distinctly raisiny-molasses, fruity sweetness and an almost viscous texture. The meat on the sandwich was chopped more finely than is usual in barbecue restaurants, and the combination of the small pieces and the sweet raisiny sauce gave the sandwich a taste leaning toward mincemeat; not bad, just unusual.

The meat on the ribs is well-done and tender, with a nice charry edge, and I can nibble my way through four in no time. The sauce seems to accompany the ribs better than the sandwich, perhaps because on ribs the serving sauce lies atop the rib in a thin layer, while on a sandwich it permeates the pile of chopped meat.

German chocolate cake and carrot cake, sliced from towering edifices, are each moist and delicious, the spicy carrot cake chock full of pecans and threads of carrot.

—*Frederic Koeppel is food critic for the* Memphis Commercial-Appeal.

Leach Family Restaurant
694 Madison at Orleans
(901-521-0867)
Hours: Monday-Friday, 11:00 A.M.–5:30 P.M.

By Frederic Koeppel

If body and soul are mystically and inextricably bound, then soul food must be an essential element of human existence. A good place to indulge in this spirit-soothing and often tongue-tantalizing cuisine is the Leach Family Restaurant. The large, spare room, once home to the fledgling Neely's Bar-B-Q, is packed at lunch. By 1:00 P.M. the kitchen begins to run out of popular dishes.

As most soul-food establishments do, the Leach Family Restaurant features such items as turkey necks, ham hocks, and buffalo fish, and liberal sprinklings of black pepper on the vegetables.

Fried chicken is offered Monday through Thursday, and it's a good thing, too, because Leach's fried chicken is excellent: moist, tender, flavorful, spicy, crisp but not too crisp, and absolutely not greasy. Two pieces will seem not enough at the time.

The spicy spaghetti, lively with pepper, is about the best of the soul-food variety I have encountered. Also terrific is what the menu terms "creamed potatoes," actually chunks of boiled potatoes served with a thick, potatoey sauce. You could bypass dessert and concentrate, instead, on the intense candied yams. I like a heaping bowl of peach cobbler much better than the banana pudding, which seems to contain more vanilla wafers than either bananas or pudding.

—*Frederic Koeppel is food critic for the* Memphis Commercial-Appeal.

Monteagle

Jim Oliver's Smokehouse Restaurant
Monteagle Exit, Interstate 24
(931-924-2268)
Hours: Open daily, 7:00 A.M.–9:00 P.M.

Jim Oliver has a regular cottage industry going—literally. There are cottages (or cabins), a campground, a gift shop, a swimming pool shaped like a ham, and one of the best restaurants you'll find so close to the interstate.

For more than twenty years, Oliver has been using his mama's know-how in the kitchen with his daddy's secrets of dry curing and hickory smoking to pack in more than a half-million visitors annually. A typical buffet lunch might include ribs, fried catfish, sliced tomatoes, corn fritters, country ham, green beans, corn, and more. During the summer months, Oliver gets his fresh vegetables from local farmers. If you time your visit right, say around July, you may be fortunate enough to get blackberries, corn on the cob, green beans, and squash fresh from the garden. Oliver also uses real potatoes, not instant ones, and the desserts (banana pudding, chocolate cream pie, and German chocolate cake) are made from family recipes. As my friend Kent Mitchell said after a visit to the Smokehouse, "Everybody knows calories don't count when you're out of town."

The atmosphere in the lodge-like restaurant is antique-rustic. Old appliances, furniture, and farm items are used to decorate the dining area.

Murfreesboro

City Cafe
113 East Main Street
(615-893-1303)
Hours: Monday-Saturday, 6:00 A.M.–7:30 P.M.

Consistency is the key to the success of the City Cafe. Garry and Pat Simpson make sure regulars are greeted cordially and the service is prompt, and cook Mary Waters takes care of the rest. Mary has been cooking breakfasts and meat-and-three lunches for customers on the square for more than two decades. Her specialties are fried catfish, turkey and dressing, roast beef and gravy, and fried chicken. The choice of vegetables is typically Southern: white beans and corn bread, baby limas, macaroni and cheese, turnip greens, candied yams, potato salad, and green beans.

Breakfast at the City Cafe is akin to watching the McLaughlin Report or Firing Line on television. This is when the professional and amateur politicians gather for biscuits and gravy and country ham and enough coffee to float the *Titanic*. No one is sure if any of the pressing political problems are ever solved, but no one leaves hungry.

By the way, the desserts are fabulous, especially the yellow cake with chocolate sauce.

Nashville

Photo by Jim Auchmutey
Biscuits and red-eye gravy at the Loveless Cafe

Loveless Cafe
Highway 100
(615-646-9700)
Hours: Daily from 8:00 A.M.–9:00 P.M.

The Loveless Cafe, which used to be part of the now-closed Loveless Motel, is as much a tradition in Nashville as The Grand Ol' Opry. In

Photo by Jim Auchmutey
*Donna McCabe, owner of the
Loveless Cafe.*

fact, on any given day, you're liable to find two or three country-music stars at the Loveless. If they aren't there, you can check out their pictures on the walls.

But stargazing is not the reason folks go to the Loveless Cafe. They go there for the biscuits and country ham and the blackberry and peach preserves and the red-eye gravy and other good things to eat. The fried chicken is no slouch, either, but your best bet is to come here for a country-ham breakfast, loosen your belt, and prepare to dip a few of those heavenly biscuits in a bowl of red-eye gravy. Oh, and save a few for buttering and preserves or sorghum syrup. And don't worry about running out of biscuits. They'll keep bringing hot ones as long as you can eat them.

Satsuma Tea Room

417 Union Street
(615-256-5211)
Hours: Monday-Friday, 10:45 A.M.–2:00 P.M.

The Satsuma Tea Room has been a downtown Nashville institution for businessmen, politicians, and ladies who lunch since 1918. The new owners since the mid-1990s are Mary Donahue, who was a waitress at the Satsuma for twenty-three years, and her sons John and Mike Donahue. Mike bakes the light and buttery yeast rolls, and John handles the cash register up front. Otherwise, little has changed. Not even the customers, some of whom have been coming here for decades. But apparently there's a new generation, too. One older waitress happily greeted a young woman who brought in her new baby for inspection.

The Satsuma's decor can only be described as cheery. The walls are bright yellow with a sunflower mural, and the well-worn antique wooden tables provide a solid, comforting feeling as you write your lunch choice on the green order ticket. Even the food is comforting. I had salmon patties with green-pea sauce, oven-browned potatoes, and garden salad with French dressing. Other choices were liver and onions, roast leg of lamb, turkey chow mein on fried noodles, or chopped country ham on homemade bread with cream of potato/ celery soup. On another day I could have gotten pork chops with homemade

Mary and John Donahue of Satsuma Tea Room

dressing, ground-beef stroganoff, Satsuma fried chicken, turnip greens, and blackberry cobbler.

For dessert, there's the ubiquitous banana pudding (but good), almond ice-box pudding, chocolate cake with ice cream and chocolate sauce, or chess pie. The homemade ice cream is wonderful with everything, except maybe the liver and onions.

Varallo's

239 4th Avenue North and 817 Church
   Street
(615-256-1907/615-256-9109)
Hours: Monday-Friday, 6:00 A.M.–2:30 P.M.

Varallo's at 817 Church Street is the oldest restaurant in Nashville. Founder Frank Varallo, Sr., opened the eating establishment at 708 Broadway in 1907 and moved to Church Street in 1919. Although Varallo's serves a full menu

Frank Varallo, Jr.

and daily specials on a cafeteria line, the restaurant is best known for its chili.

Frank, Sr., began serving the chili at the Climax Saloon. He had traveled around the world as a violinist early in life and in his travels to South America he picked up a chili recipe that four generations have cooked. There are stories that the chili was so hot that you had to be drunk to eat it. Later, he toned down the spices to appeal to a broader base.

The restaurant on Church Street is now run by Frank Varallo, Jr., while two grandsons, Todd and Tony Varallo, have taken over a new location on Fourth Avenue. The menu— and the chili—are the same at both places. Plate lunches include country-fried steak, fried chicken, chicken and dressing, chicken and dumplings,

Todd and Kristi Varallo

meat loaf, and salmon croquettes, with an assortment of Southern vegetables. The vegetables are fresh and tasty, but you need to schedule your visit during the cold months so you can try the chili. It's terrific, even if you're sober.

Newport

Tucker's Main Street Cafe

265 Main Street
(423-623-9137)
Hours: Monday-Friday, 8:00 A.M.–2:00 P.M.

Tucker's is quintessential small-town cafe, with a menu item or two not usually found in such places. Alongside the pan-fried chicken breast and the hamburger steak, there's chicken broccoli alfredo, chicken quesadilla, and a blooming onion.

There's also a daily special with vegetables—the chicken casserole, with mashed potatoes, green beans, and slaw, was wonderful. Lunch also includes the usual array of sandwiches and burgers. The Train Tracks Breakfasts (the restaurant is across the street from the depot) come with gravy. Tenderloin is a breakfast option, too.

Pigeon Forge

Apple Tree Inn

3215 Parkway
(423-453-4961)
Hours: Daily from 6:30 A.M.–10:00 P.M.

If you've never been to Pigeon Forge, you're in for a treat or a nightmare, depending on how much you thrive on touristy spots. There's a huge outlet mall here and lots of other attractions for out-of-town visitors. During the peak season, which seems to be about any time of the year, but particularly in the summer and fall, the roads can get pretty congested. But if you find yourself in Pigeon Forge anyway and you're feeling hungry, stop in at the Apple Tree Inn. That's the place with the original anvil from the iron forge that gave the town half its name. For thirty years, owner Garnet Cole has been serving home-cooked meals family style. That means all you have to do is sit down at a table and they'll bring you your sweet tea and three meats, four vegetables, and dessert. You don't have to get up and go through a buffet line. You can order trout or other items from the menu, but most customers are satisfied with the steak and gravy, fried chicken, barbecue ribs, meat loaf, mashed potatoes, greens, and peas. And anybody who has ever eaten there will tell you to save room for the homemade peach, apple, or cherry cobblers.

Sharp's Chapel

Cole's Store
Corner of Leadmine Bend and Edwards Hollow Roads
Hours: Monday–Sunday, 7:00 A.M.–8:00 P.M.

Cole's is one of those rural places where there's a little bit of everything on the shelves. The menu is limited to a few sandwiches. Bologna is $1.00, with cheese $1.40. The fanciest sandwich is corned beef. Get your bologna sandwich and a cold "dope" (a soft drink) from the box and go to the back table and watch the ongoing card game. Ongoing, say some of the regulars, for years. Or, if the weather's nice, you might want to wander outside and join the whittlers on the bench beside the front door, where you'll hear a funny story about the card game and the players.

VIRGINIA

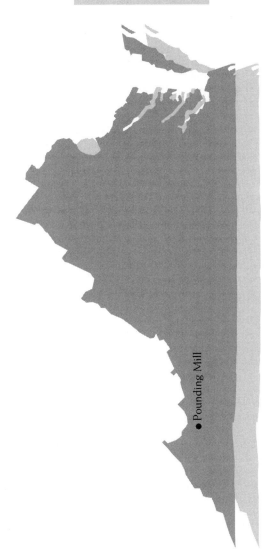

Pounding Mill

Note from the publisher: For a comprehensive listing of restaurants in Virginia, see *Small-Town Restaurants in Virginia* by Joanne M. Anderson. However, Lee Smith submitted a description of her favorite restaurant, which just happens to be located in Virginia. Although it is the only Virginia restaurant included in this book, we had to include it because Lee's description was so much fun.

Pounding Mill

Other Voices, Other Tastes

Cuz's Uptown Barbecue

Lee Smith

"This is hit!" proclaims the hand-lettered sign on a rickety wooden fence. "This is *what?*" you're likely to wonder as you zip past on southwest Virginia's Route 460. You slow down to get a good look at the old silo and the red ramshackle dairy barn with CUZ'S spray-painted on its fluorescent yellow door. Outbuildings abound. Several of them appear to have dancing pigs and hearts on them . . . but, no, wait, that's a *dragon* . . . and what's that up on the hill? a *tennis court?* You almost wreck the car, looking. But you don't stop. Nobody in his right mind would stop there unless he knew where he was going.

And the only way he'd know is word of mouth, because the owners, Mike and Yvonne Thompson, don't advertise this establishment, easily the most eccentric eatery in Virginia: Cuz's Uptown Barbecue of Pounding Mill. That's right up the road from Claypool Hill, folks, just beyond Richlands on Route 460, heading toward Bluefield.

They don't *need* to advertise. Regulars drive to the restaurant from a seventy-five-mile radius; and longer "Cuz runs" have become such a phenomenon that Mike and Yvonne recently built two gorgeous hand-hewn log cabins—complete with jacuzzies, satellite TVs, fireplaces, and CD players, along with a little kidney-shaped pool—to catch the overflow of long-distance diners. Last year the restaurant served twenty thousand steaks and used five and a half tons of flour for baking. Every Friday and Saturday night, three or four hundred people show up.

They can enjoy live bluegrass, plus beer or a glass of wine, upstairs in the "Elvis and Cows" lounge while they wait for a table, or just relax and take in a show and the wild decor. It's a world-class people-watching opportunity, too, as coal barons rub elbows with good ol' boys and egghead professors from the community college down the road. Everybody seems to know everybody—or they *will*, before long—and you will, too, if you stay long enough. In terms of dress code, the idea seems to be, *go for it!* You'll see everything here from gold lamé to overalls.

"The basic decorating scheme is pigs in paradise," Mike Thompson, age forty-eight, says. There's also a lot of Elvis, including a great lamp with a lighted globe on top of his head, a wooden life-size cut-out in the entrance and another one upstairs, cavorting with cows. Tiny Tim, Pee Wee Herman, and Freddy Krueger are also featured. At first you're thinking, "Well! This is certainly the tackiest place I've ever been in" . . . but then you *get* it. Folk art! This whole place is folk art, a masterpiece.

Sure enough, country boy Mike (it was his family's dairy farm) picked up an art degree from Vanderbilt before he took up the spatula. Yvonne, born in Hong Kong, came to Richlands originally to work on the local newspaper. Oriental touches—like that dragon or menu items such as the Tuna Teriyaki or the Thai Seafood Curry with Filet Satays, reflect her influence.

But the big thing at Cuz's is the beef—and I mean *big!* The large prime rib is a twenty-five-ounce cut called a "Hunka Hunka." The house specialty is Smoked Prime Rib with Burgundy Gravy; you can't go wrong with the Green Peppercorn Filet, either. The prize-winning Acapulco Filet is a towering tenderloin steak combination involving sautéed hot and sweet peppers, grilled onion ringlets, garlic molé sauce with portobello mushrooms, sweet salsa with avocado, and cilantro . . .you get the picture. Or you could go exotic, try the smoked emu or maybe the ostrich—imagine finding all this in southwest Virginia! When I was growing up around here, the best you could do at a local restaurant was a sausage biscuit, or maybe a gray hamburger steak and green beans or pintos cooked all day long, just like Mama's.

Mike's barbecue comes any way you want it—beef, pork, pork ribs, or a three-way platter, all slow-roasted outside in a wood-fired milk-cooler-turned-pig-cooker, then oven-baked in a tomato-based sauce.

Other entrées are eclectic and ever-changing: lobsters flown in from Maine, catfish flown in from Mississippi, trout mousse, grilled wild mushrooms with saffron cream on pasta, charbroiled quails with pepper jelly and garlic sauce—whatever Mike feels like cooking that day. All entrées are served with a garden salad, homemade French bread, made right there, and your choice of baked potato, fries, or rice.

Since the portions are huge, some people make a meal out of appetizers, which include hot crabmeat-cheese dip, fried stuffed jalapeño peppers, and eggrolls. Desserts tend to be large and comforting, such as strawberry shortcake and peach cobbler, though there's also a nice tart little Key lime pie.

I will lie down and die for the crabcakes with chili hollandaise sauce, which comes as an appetizer or entrée. It's real hard for me to order anything else.

Prices range from $8.50 to $22.00. Cuz's is open Wednesday through Sunday only, from 3:00-9:00 P.M (later on the weekend), March through December only—Mike and Yvonne take a two-month break, and usually a quick trip to the Orient—before they crank it all up again.

So now you know. Next time you're passing through, pull over. Let out your belt a notch or two and join Elvis in paradise.

Lee Smith is a North Carolina writer. She is the author of several books, including *Fair and Tender Ladies*, *Family Linen*, and *News of the Spirit*.

Index